PREHISTORIC ORIGAMI

MARC KIRSCHENBAUM

FIT TO PRINT PUBLISHING, INC.

NEW YORK, NY

ISBN 978-1-951146-19-1 (Paperback Edition)
ISBN 978-1-951146-20-7 (Hardcover Edition)

The diagrams in this book were produced with Macromedia's Freehand, and image processing was done with Adobe Photoshop. The Backtalk family of typefaces was used for the body text and the headers use Helvetica. Prehistoric Regular was used for the cover. Ellen Cohen assisted with the cover design and provided valuable artistic assistance.

Contents

Introduction

Ancient fossils and bones have captured the imaginations of artists around the world. Fleshing out the often-incomplete excavated skeletons has created controversy, pushing the limits of our understanding of how prehistoric creatures have evolved. Most reconstructions take a skin-tight approach to the animal's form, but perhaps there are some softer tissues not accounted for that would drastically affect the creature's shape? The color of these animal's skin has also been in question. While many dinosaurs are related to modern reptiles, they are also related to modern birds. So, it is possible that their skin can be any number of colors, and for that matter be largely covered by feathers.

Abstraction is the best approach for realizing these questionable creatures, and origami by nature is great at obfuscating details. This collection of twelve origami pieces celebrates the animals that existed before man took over the planet. Each piece is designed to be folded from commonly available origami papers. While all of them can ultimately be folded from the six-inch (fifteen centimeter) variety, it might be best to practice with the larger ten-inch (twenty-five centimeter) papers. Be creative with your color and pattern selection of paper, especially since we are not sure how these animals looked anyway.

Dinosaurs are well represented in this selection, including favorites like the *Stegosaurus* and *Triceratops*. The *T-rex Skeleton* features the popular predator's frame constructed from four squares of paper linked together. You can use your imagination to decide which species the *Fossil* and frivolous *Dino Hatchling* corresponds to.

There are lots of popular creatures from well before the dinosaurs appeared, so a *Dimetrodon* and *Trilobite* are included. To represent some of the favorite mammals that came after the dinosaur's tenure, a cartoonish *Sabre-Toothed Tiger* and *Woolly Mammoth* round out this collection.

To ease you through, the models are roughly ordered by their difficulty level. If you find a particular sequence challenging, perhaps consider trying a larger paper to practice with. Also taking a break from folding can often work wonders. Most importantly, have fun recreating these works!

Paper & Materials

Picking the perfect paper for your origami project can range from fun to frustrating. There are many origami designs with well over a hundred steps that demand specialty papers that can handle their stressful folding sequences. Fortunately, all these simpler pieces can be made from almost any paper made for origami. While it might be tempting to just use copy paper (or any scrap paper lying around), often such materials are too thick to handle more than a few layers of folds.

One of the better varieties to consider is kami, which is the Japanese word for *paper*. It is often just simply sold as *origami paper*, being extremely common. It can be found on most online stores, hobby shops, and of course origami stores (such as The Source, which is part of OrigamiUSA). The standard size is six inches (or fifteen centimeters) which is suitable for these projects. You could also consider the larger ten-inch size (or twenty-five-centimeter variety), especially for the models with more detail. Once you are comfortable with the folding sequence, you can work your way towards using the smaller papers.

Most kami papers sport a decorative side (either plain or patterned) with the other side being plain white. A few of the models showcase both sides of the paper, so you should consider the *duo* or *double-sided* variety of kami. Of course, stay clear from the papers that are simply the same color on both sides.

Other papers sold for origami purposes are not as easy to work with. Foil backed papers do look nice and shiny when they are pristine, but they will pick up any extraneous creases as you fold. Some sequences call for changing a valley fold to a mountain fold, and foil papers a notoriously inflexible at that task. Washi papers are typically very durable, but do not often hold a crease well without special treatment. One solution is to use glue while folding, with PVA adhesives being ideal.

More adventurous folders might consider custom paper preparations. This can be as simple as using a favorite giftwrap and cutting it down to size. If you are considering getting a paper cutter, rotary style is more accurate and far safer than the guillotine kind. A popular European wrapping paper variety is known as *kraft* paper, which is the German word for *strong*. Most origami shops will sell it precut into squares. Unfortunately, like most wrapping paper, it is plain on the other side. Some origami artists will paint their papers with watered down acrylic paints.

A less messy approach is to glue a lightweight sheet onto the other side. A perfect adhesive for this application is methylcellulose, often abbreviated as *MC*. MC comes in a powder form that needs to be mixed into cold water. About two teaspoons per 1.5 cups of water is a good ratio. After about thirty minutes of periodic stirring the MC will reach a syrupy consistency. It can be brushed on your paper (any cheap paintbrush is fine) after which you can place your thinner paper atop. You can then brush more MC for a better bond. The drying process can be accelerated with a table fan. Many of the models showcased here were prepared with this technique. Have fun experimenting with different materials.

Symbols & Terminology

Valley Fold

A dashed line with an open-headed arrow indicates to *Valley Fold* (fold forward in the direction of the arrow).

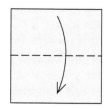 

1. Valley fold in half.   2. Completed *Valley Fold*.

Mountain Fold

A dashed line with dots along with a closed-headed arrow indicates to *Mountain Fold* (fold behind in the direction of the arrow).

1. Mountain fold in half.   2. Completed *Mountain Fold*.

Precrease

A valley fold line with a double-headed arrow indicates to Precrease (valley fold and then unfold in the direction of the open headed arrow). The resulting *crease* is represented by a thin line.

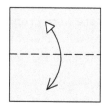 

1. Precrease in half.   2. Completed *Precrease*.

Turn Over

Turn over is indicated by a looped arrow.

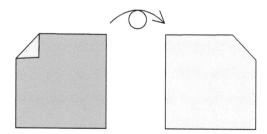

Rotate

Rotate is indicated by a circle with arrows along it.

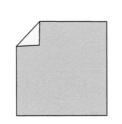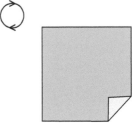

Hidden / Imaginary Lines

Hidden/Imaginary lines are indicated by a thin dotted line.

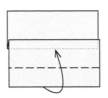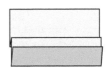

1. Valley fold to the hidden edge.
2. Completed fold.

Angle Bisectors

Open dots are sometimes used to indicate angle bisectors.

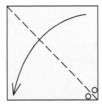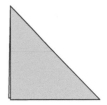

1. Valley fold along the indicated angle bisector.
2. Completed fold.

Divided Brackets

A divided bracket with tick marks shows equal divisions.

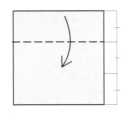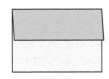

1. Valley fold along the 1/3rd mark.
2. Completed *Valley Fold*.

Reference Dots

Dots are sometimes used to call attention to a specific landmark.

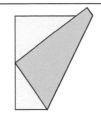

1. Valley fold the dotted corner to the dotted crease.
2. Completed fold.

Pleat Fold

A *Pleat Fold* is indicated by a mountain fold line followed by a valley fold line. An arrow indicates the direction of the pleat.

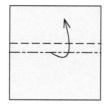 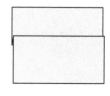

1. Pleat fold upwards.

2. Completed *Pleat Fold*.

Reverse Fold

A solid arrow indicates to push in or invert at the indicated area for a *Reverse Fold*, *Squash Fold* or various types of *Sink Folds*. For a *Reverse Fold*, you invert the indicated section.

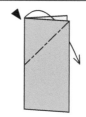 

1. Reverse fold the corner.

2. Completed *Reverse Fold*.

Squash Fold

A *Squash Fold* is a combination of a reverse fold with opening out the inverted area.

1. Squash fold the corner.

2. Completed *Squash Fold*.

Sink Fold

A *Sink Fold* is related to a reverse fold, but it is performed on a point from the middle of the paper. After precreasing where this fold occurs, you open out the point and invert it along the perimeter of the creases.

1. Sink fold the corner.

2. Completed *Sink Fold*.

Closed Sink

Sink folds can also be formed without fully opening out the connecting layers. This is called a *Closed Sink*.

1. Closed Sink fold the corner.

2. Completed *Closed Sink*.

Sink Triangularly

A hybrid version (half open and half closed) is called *Sinking Triangularly*.

1. Sink fold the corner triangularly.

2. Completed *Sink Fold*.

Petal Fold

A *Petal Fold* is indicated by an open headed arrow with squash fold arrows. A layer is raised up, causing side edges to get pulled inwards and squash folded flat.

1. Petal fold the corner.

2. Completed *Petal Fold*.

Outside Reverse Fold

An *Outside Reverse Fold* is indicated by a set of arrows. You wrap around the indicated layer and flatten.

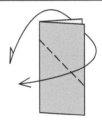

1. Outside reverse fold the corner.

2. Completed *Outside Reverse Fold*.

Crimp Fold

A *Crimp Fold* is indicated by a set of arrows. It is sometimes accompanied with a sink arrow or a set of zigzag lines to show how the layers are distributed. You spread apart the sides of a flap and form a set of valley and mountain folds on each side to change the position of the tip. There are a number of variations on this fold.

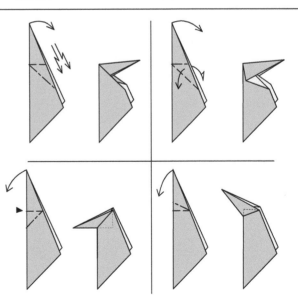

Spread Squash

A *Spread Squash* is a sink fold that is spread open.

1. Spread squash the corner.

2. Completed *Spread Squash*.

Unsink

A hollow arrow is used to show an area to be unsunk or where layers would be pulled out.

1. Unsink the corner.

2. Completed *Unsink*.

Swivel Fold

Swivel Fold is indicated by a set of arrows and sometimes accompanied with a sink arrow. Edges are folded over in two different areas, while the connecting paper is squash folded flat.

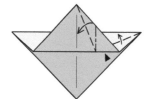

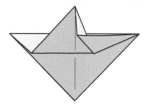

1. Swivel fold the corner.

2. Completed *Swivel Fold*.

Rabbit Ear

Rabbit Ear is indicated by a set of arrows. Two edges are valley folded in, while the connecting paper is pinched flat into a new flap.

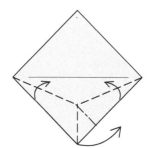

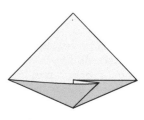

1. Rabbit ear the corner.

2. Completed *Rabbit Ear*.

Brontosaurus

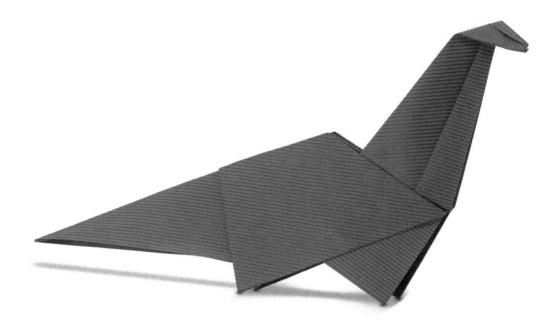

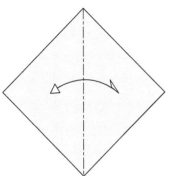

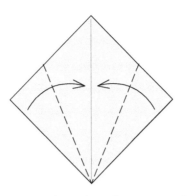

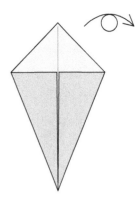

1. Precrease along the diagonal
   with a mountain fold.

2. Valley fold the sides to the center.

3. Turn over.

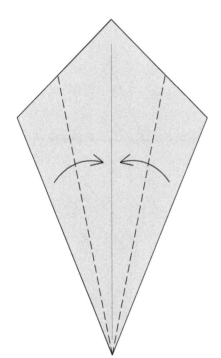

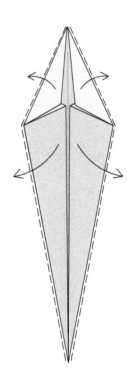

4. Valley fold the sides to the center.

5. Valley fold the sides, noting they
   will *not* meet at the center.

6. Open out the sides (undoing the
   last two steps).

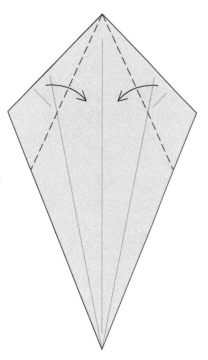

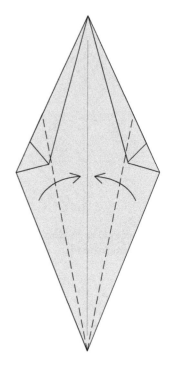

7. Valley fold the sides inwards by extending the existing creases.

8. Valley fold the sides outwards.

9. Valley fold the sides to the center again.

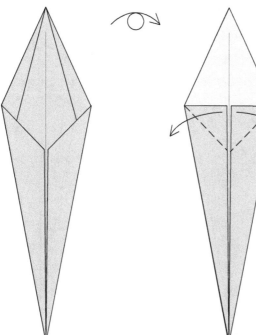

10. Turn over.

11. Valley fold the corners outwards so the sides lie straight.

12. Open out the sides.

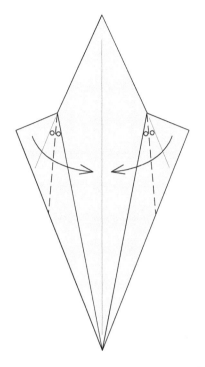

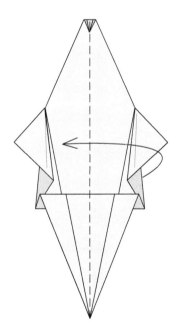

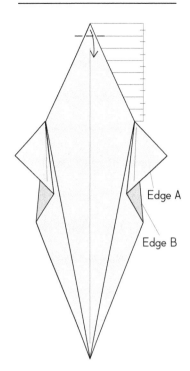

Edge A

Edge B

13. Valley fold the sides back in along the indicated angle bisectors.

14. Valley fold the corners outwards so that the resulting inner edges are equal (Edge A and B from the next step).

15. Valley fold the tip in at about 1/8th the indicated height.

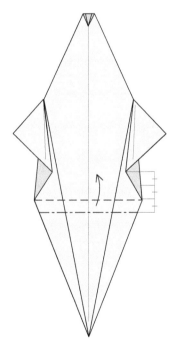

16. Pleat the bottom flap upwards along the suggested division point..

17. Valley fold in half.

18. Pleat the neck. See the next step for suggested positioning.

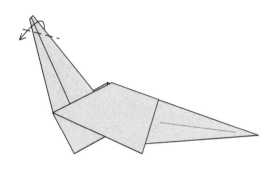

19. Wrap the body layer around the pleat in the neck. Rotate the model.

20. Valley fold a little bit of the flap down.

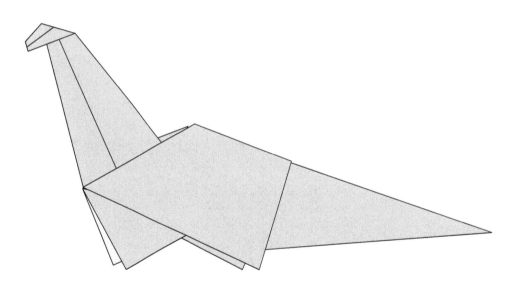

21. Completed *Brontosaurus*.

Trilobite

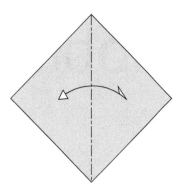
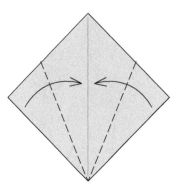
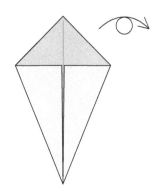

1. Precrease along the diagonal with a mountain fold.

2. Valley fold the sides to the center.

3. Turn over.

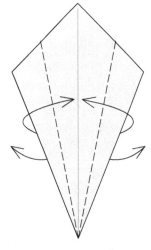
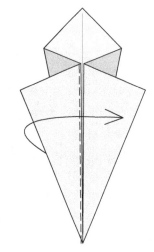
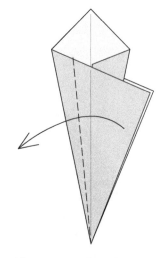

4. Valley fold the sides to the center allowing the flaps from behind to swing forward.

5. Swing over one layer.

6. Valley fold over along the angle bisector.

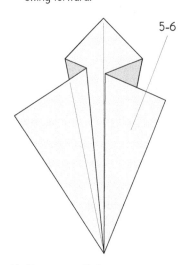
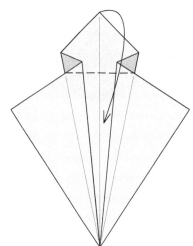
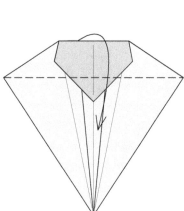

7. Repeat steps 5-6 in mirror image.

8. Valley fold the top section down.

9. Valley fold down again.

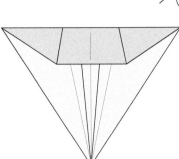

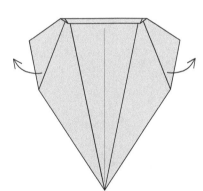

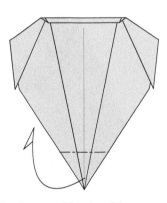

10. Turn over.

11. Valley fold down so the side edges are aligned.

12. Mountain fold the sides behind.

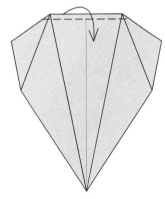

13. Valley fold a little bit of the edge over.

14. Slide the side flaps outwards slightly.

15. Mountain fold a bit of the tip behind.

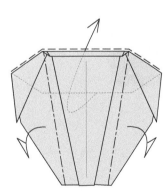

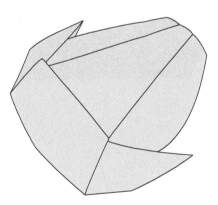

16. Open out the hidden bottom edge, curling the sides into a 3-D shape.

17. Completed *Trilobite*.

Fossil

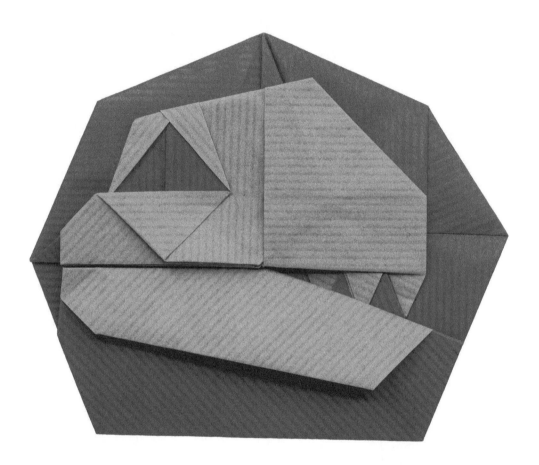

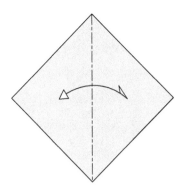

1. Precrease along the diagonal with a mountain fold.

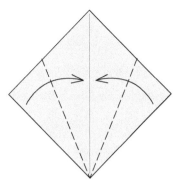

2. Valley fold the sides to the center.

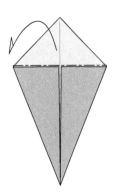

3. Mountain fold the corner behind.

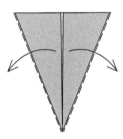

4. Open out the sides.

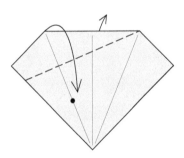

5. Valley fold the corner to the dotted crease. Allow the flap from behind to flip out.

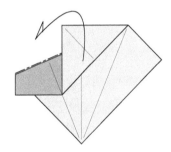

6. Swing the flap back to the previous position.

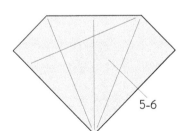

7. Repeat steps 5-6 in mirror image.

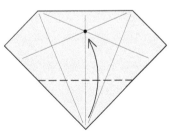

8. Valley fold the corner to the dotted intersection of creases.

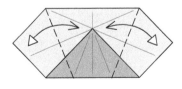

9. Precrease along the existing creases (adding new folds on the top flap).

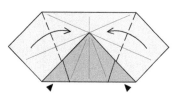

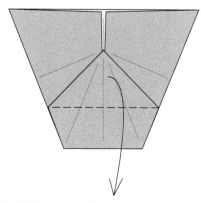

10. Reverse fold along the existing creases.

11. Valley fold the corner down.

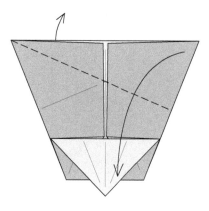

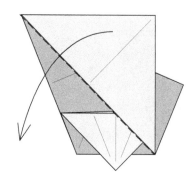

12. Valley fold towards the bottom corner, allowing the rear flap to flip out.

13. Swing over the top flap.

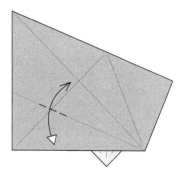

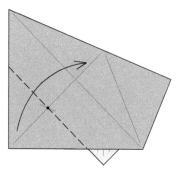

14. Precrease the middle along the angle bisector.

15. Valley fold through the dotted intersection of creases.

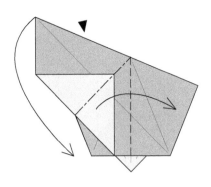

16. Squash fold over along the center.

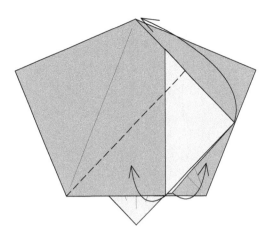

17. Bring the corner to the top, allowing the sides to spread apart and lie flat.

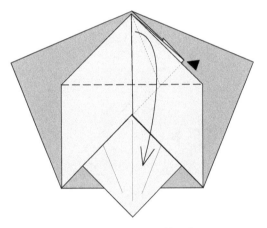

18. Valley fold down, allowing the hidden flap to squash fold flat.

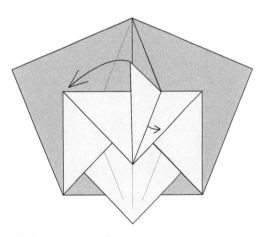

19. Pull out the trapped corner.

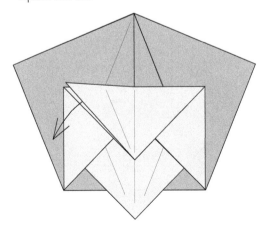

20. Pull out the middle layer.

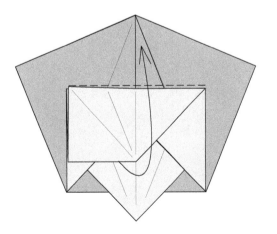

21. Swing the flap up.

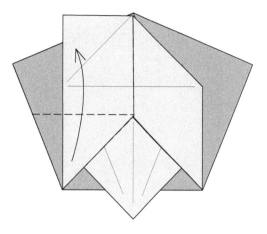

22. Valley fold the flap up.

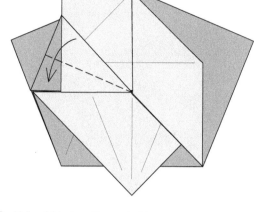

23. Valley fold along the angle bisector.

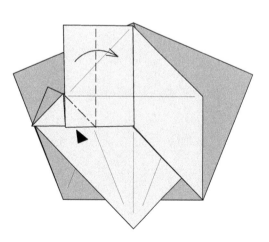

24. Swing the flap down.

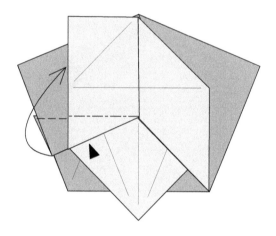

25. Reverse fold the flap up.

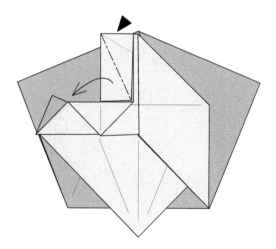

26. Valley fold over while squash folding the corner.

27. Squash fold the flap.

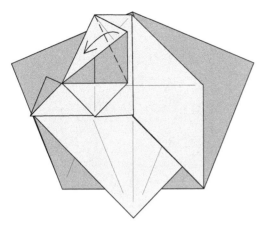

28. Valley fold the flap over.

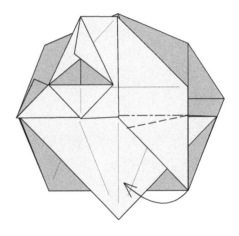

29. Mountain fold the corner.

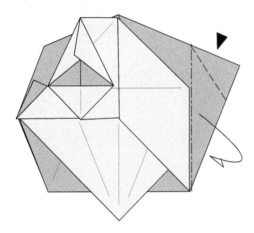

30. Swivel fold the side inside.

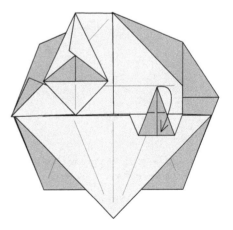

31. Pleat the flap so it lies symmetrically.

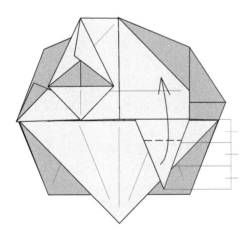

32. Valley fold up, starting a small amount above 1/3rd the height of the flap.

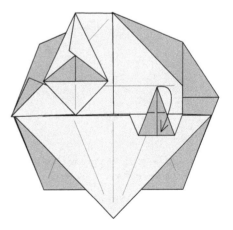

33. Valley fold the corner to the bottom edge.

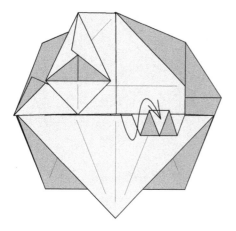

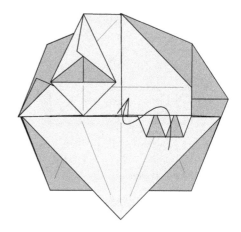

34. Tuck the flap underneath the top layer.

35. Bring the bottom flap to the surface.

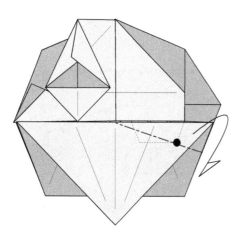

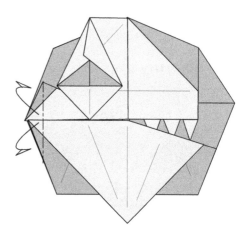

36. Mountain fold the flap so it aligns with the dotted corner of the hidden flap.

37. Mountain fold the corners inside.

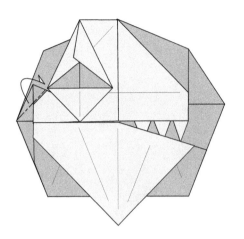 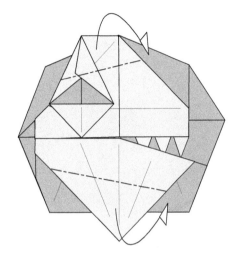

38. Mountain fold the corner inside.

39. Mountain fold the flaps inside, tapering the folds as desired.

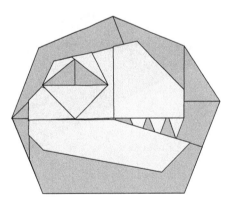

40. Completed *Fossil*.

Saber-Toothed
Tiger

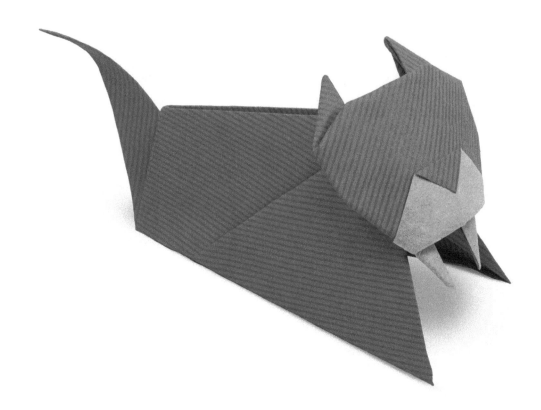

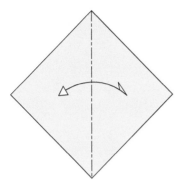

1. Precrease along the diagonal with a mountain fold.

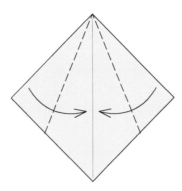

2. Valley fold the sides to the center.

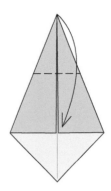

3. Valley fold down.

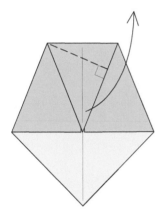

4. Valley fold the flap so its edges are aligned.

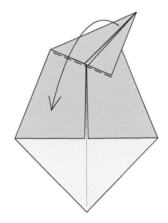

5. Swing the flap back down.

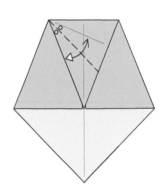

6. Precrease along the indicated angle bisector.

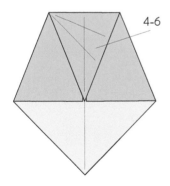

4-6

7. Repeat steps 4-6 in mirror image.

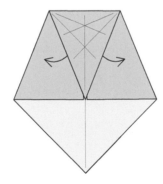

8. Using the existing creases, slide out a layer at each side so they are straight.

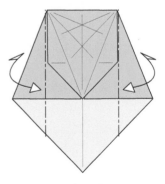

9. Precrease the sides with mountain folds. The corners should meet at the center.

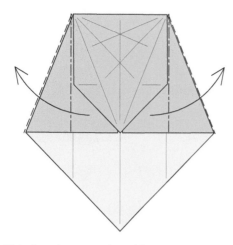

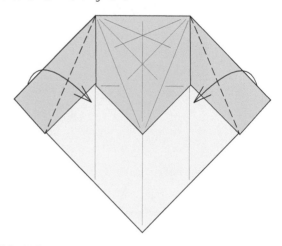

10. Slide the sides outwards and flatten.

11. Valley fold along the angle bisectors.

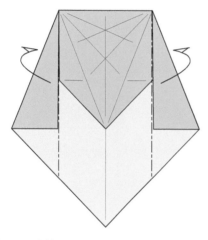

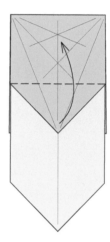

12. Mountain fold along the existing creases.

13. Valley fold the corner up.

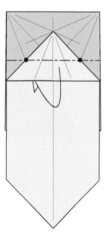

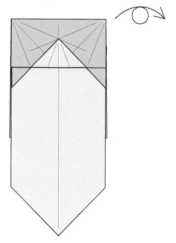

14. Mountain fold the edge inside using the dotted
    intersections.

15. Turn over.

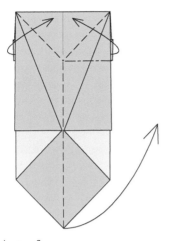

16. Rabbit ear the top flap.

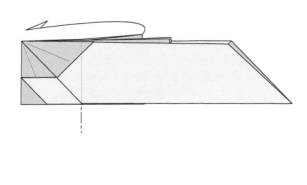

17. Swing the rear flap over.

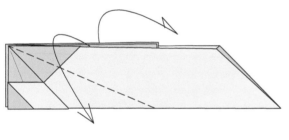

18. Outside reverse fold using the inner edges as a guide.

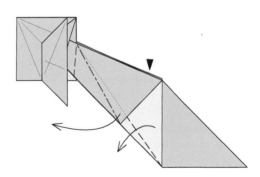

19. Valley fold the side in while swivel folding the bottom corner down.

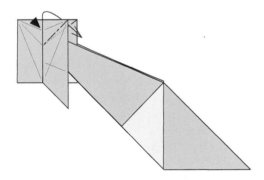

20. Reverse fold the top corner.

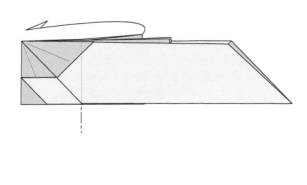

21. Squash fold the top pleated section.

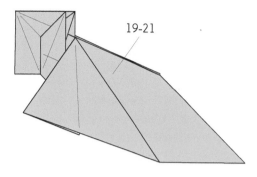

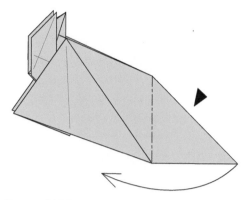

22. Repeat steps 19-21 behind.

23. Reverse fold the corner.

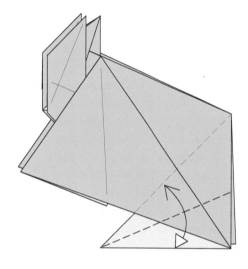

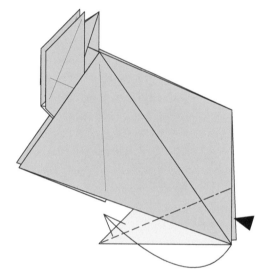

24. Precrease along the angle bisector.

25. Reverse fold the flap along the existing creases.

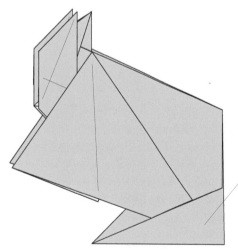

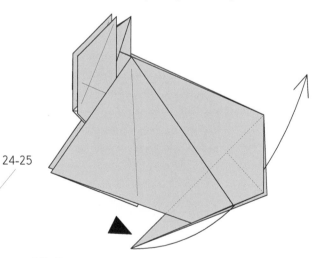

26. Repeat steps 24-25 behind.

27. Reverse fold the flap up.

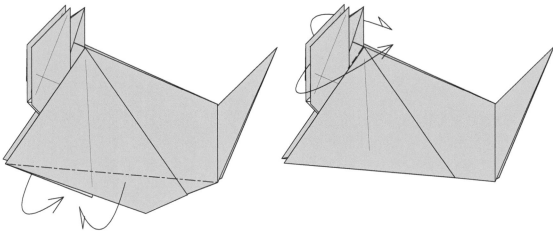

28. Mountain fold the bottom edges inside.

29. Outside reverse fold the cluster of flaps.

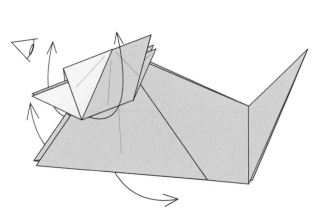

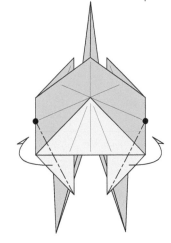

30. Spread apart the sides of the body and spread apart the head section so it is flat.

31. View from the previous step. Mountain fold the sides starting from the dotted intersections.

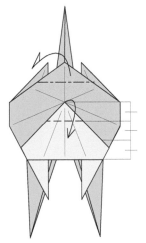

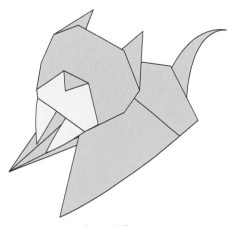

32. Valley fold and mountain fold the corners using the suggested reference points.

33. Completed *Saber-Toothed Tiger*.

Pterodactyl

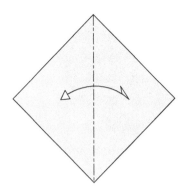

1. Precrease along the diagonal with a mountain fold.

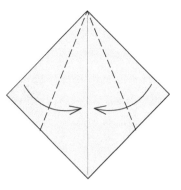

2. Valley fold the sides to the center.

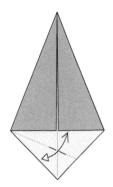

3. Precrease the middle along the angle bisector.

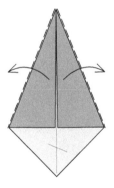

4. Unfold the sides.

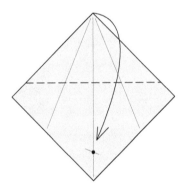

5. Valley fold to the dotted intersection of creases.

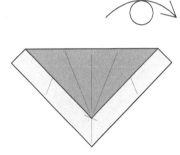

6. Turn over.

7. Valley fold the sides to the center.

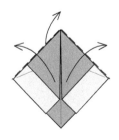

8. Unfold completely.

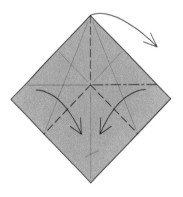

9. Rabbit ear along the existing creases.

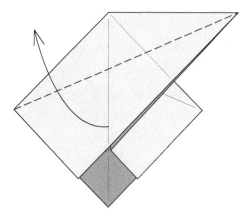

10. Valley fold the top layer up.

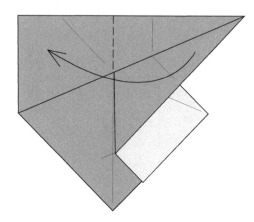

11. Swing over the center flap.

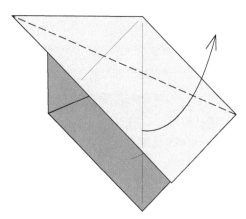

12. Valley fold the top layer up.

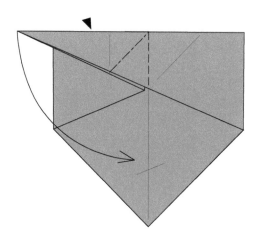

13. Squash fold the center flap down.

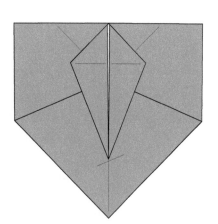

14. Turn over.

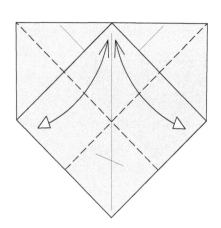

15. Precrease both sides.

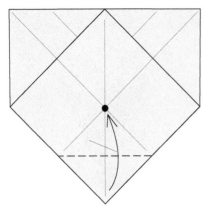

16. Valley fold to the dotted intersection of creases.

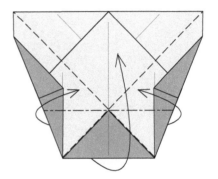

17. Precrease the sides partway.

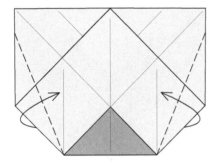

18. Valley fold the sides to the last creases.

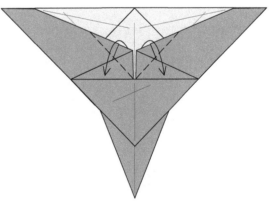

19. Fold up while reverse folding the sides.

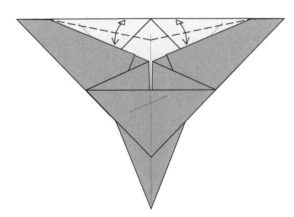

20. Precrease along the angle bisectors.

21. Valley fold towards the folded edge.

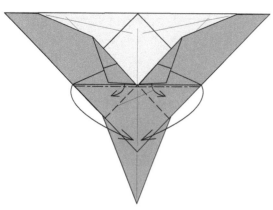

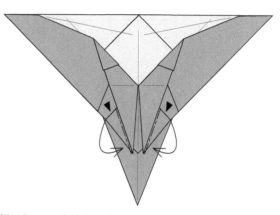

22. Valley fold the corners to the bottom, allowing the trapped paper to slide out at each side.

23. Reverse fold the sides.

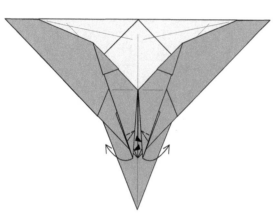

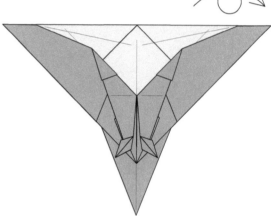

24. Squash fold the tips of the flaps. See the next steps for a suggested amount and positioning.

25. Turn over.

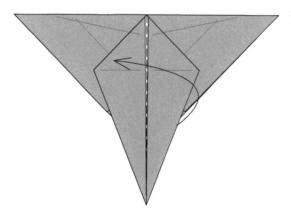

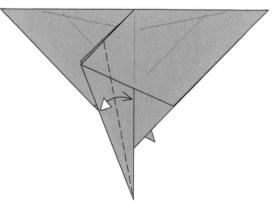

26. Swing one flap over.

27. Precrease along the angle bisector.

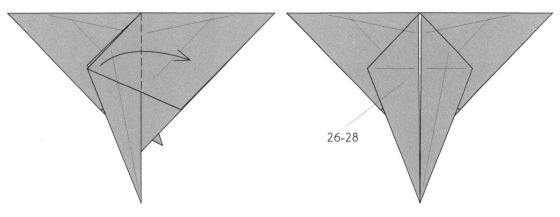

28. Swing the flap back over.

29. Repeat steps 26-28 in mirror image.

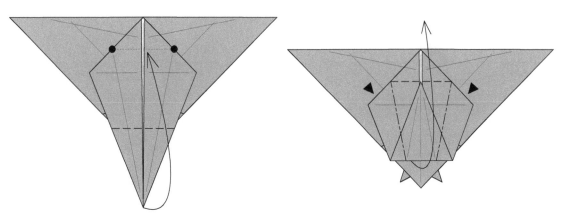

30. Valley fold to the imaginary line between the dotted intersections.

31. Bring the flap up while squash folding the sides.

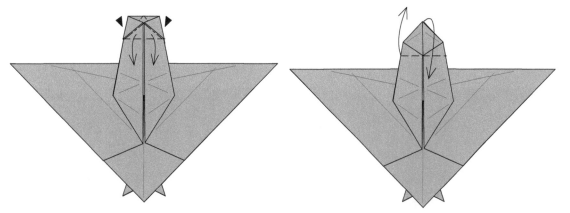

32. Squash fold the corners.

33. Valley fold down, allowing the flap from behind to flip over.

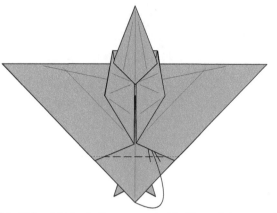

34. Valley fold the bottom corner inside. Parts of the fold are hidden.

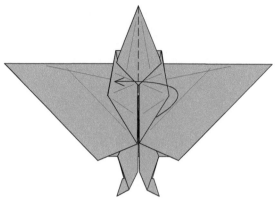

35. Swing over one flap.

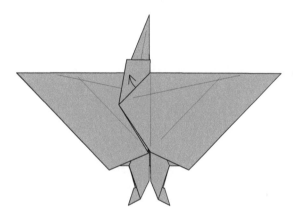

36. Pull out a single layer of trapped paper.

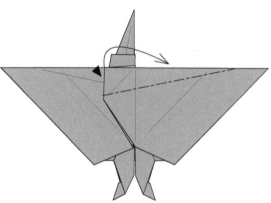

37. Reverse fold along the existing crease.

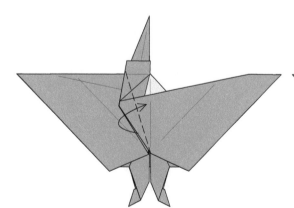

38. Valley fold along the angle bisector.

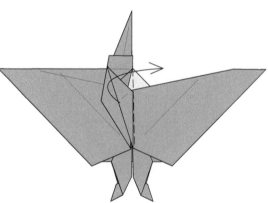

39. Swing the flap back over.

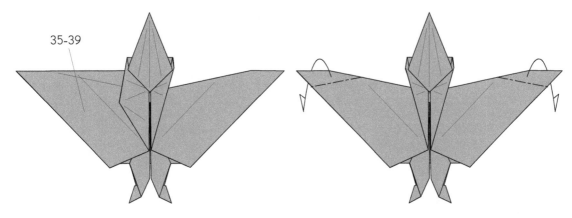

40. Repeat steps 35-39 in mirror image.

41. Mountain fold a little bit of the top edges behind.

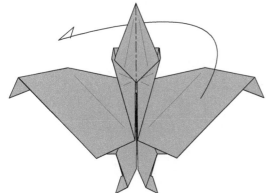

42. Mountain fold in half.

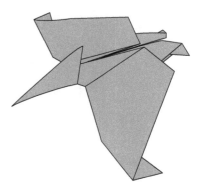

43. Pivot the top section, reforming some of the folds and flatten.

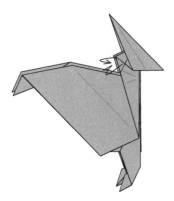

44. Mountain fold the edges inside.

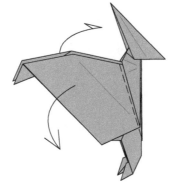

45. Valley fold the wings outwards, allowing the legs to curl down slightly and splay outwards.

46. Completed *Pterodactyl*.

Dino Hatchling

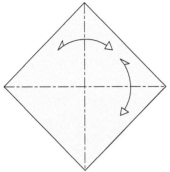

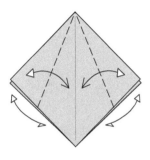

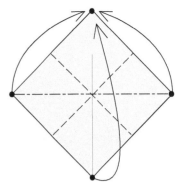

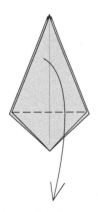

1. Precrease the diagonals with mountain folds.

2. Precrease the sides in half.

3. Collapse the corners up.

4. Precrease the sides along the angle bisectors.

5. Reverse fold the sides.

6. Swing the top flap down.

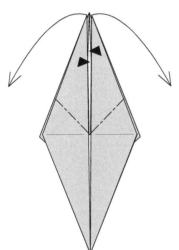

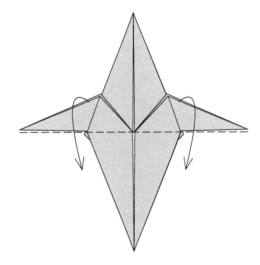

7. Reverse fold the top flaps outwards.

8. Swing down the top layers of the side flaps.

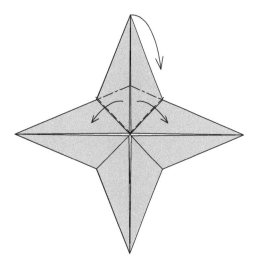

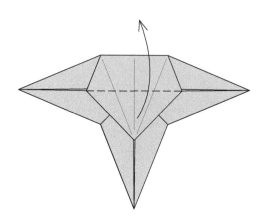

9. Spread apart the top layers of the flap while squash folding it down.

10. Valley fold the top layer up.

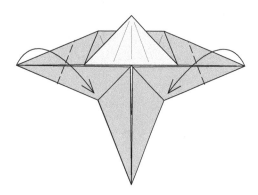

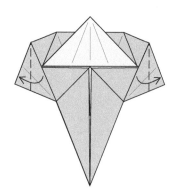

11. Valley fold the corners over.

12. Valley fold the flaps outwards.

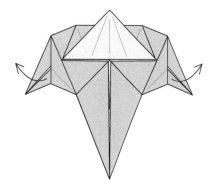

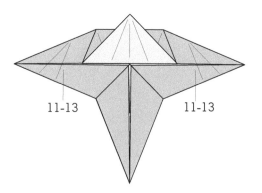

13. Unfold the side pleats.

14. Repeat steps 11-13 in the opposite direction.

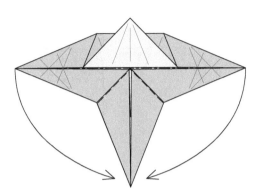

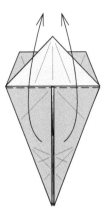

15. Pull the side flaps down, allowing them to mountain fold in half.

16. Swing the flaps up.

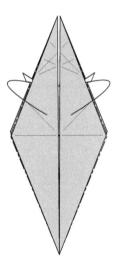

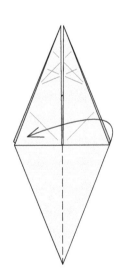

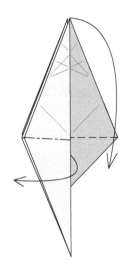

17. Wrap around a single layer at each side.

18. Swing over one flap.

19. Swing the flap down while pulling out the top layer.

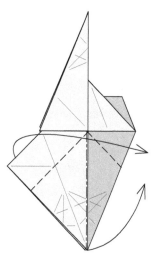

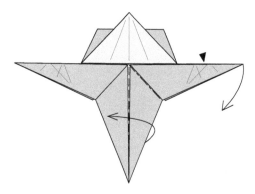

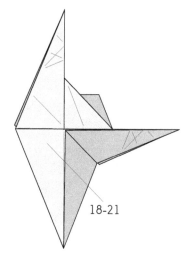

20. Swing over while reverse folding the flap over.

21. Valley fold along the angle bisectors, allowing the hidden corner to squash fold flat.

22. Repeat steps 18-21 in mirror image.

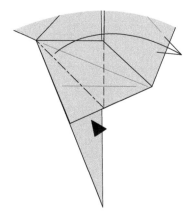

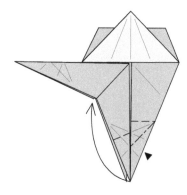

23. Squash fold the side flap down.

24. Squash fold along the existing creases.

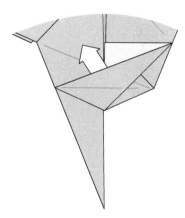

25. Squash fold the flap over.

26. Pull out a single layer and flatten.

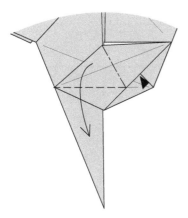

27. Squash fold the center flap down.

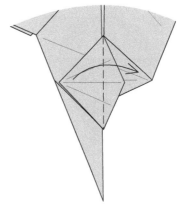

28. Valley fold the top layer over.

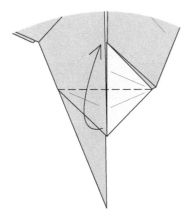

29. Valley fold the flap up.

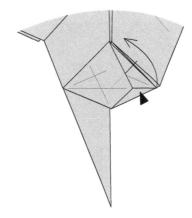

30. Reverse fold the flap up.

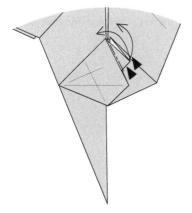

31. Reverse fold the corners.

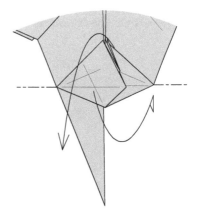

32. Swing the cluster of flaps down, allowing the bottom point to flip behind.

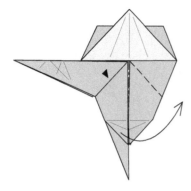

33. Squash fold the flap over.

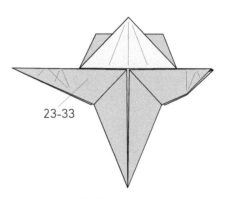

34. Repeat steps 23-33 in mirror image.

35. Valley fold towards the dotted intersections.

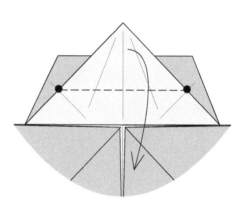

36. Valley fold starting from the dotted intersections.

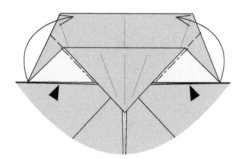

37. Reverse fold along the existing creases.

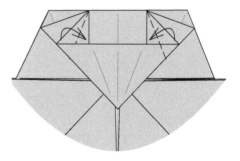

38. Valley fold along the angle bisectors.

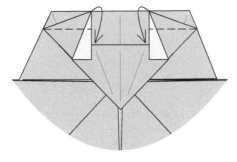 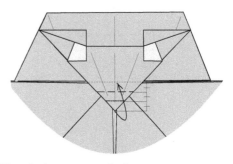

39. Valley fold the corners towards the folded edge.

40. Pleat the bottom using thirds.

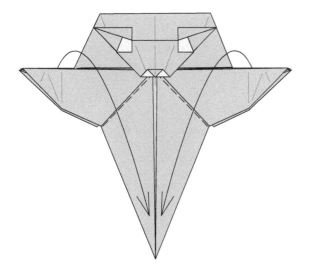 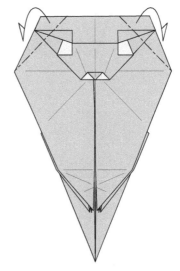

41. Swing the flaps down.

42. Mountain fold the corners.

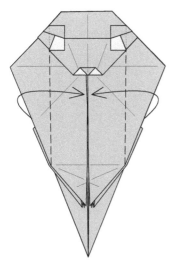 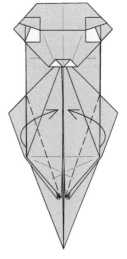

43. Valley fold the sides to the center.

44. Valley fold along the angle bisectors.

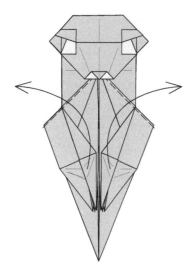

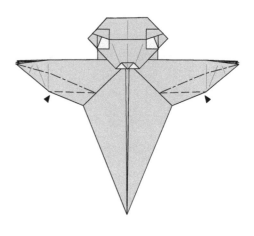

45. Swing the flaps outwards.

46. Sink the flaps along the angle bisectors.

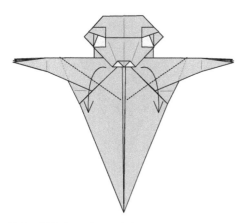

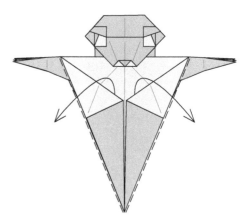

47. Valley fold along the angle bisectors.

48. Swing the top layers outwards.

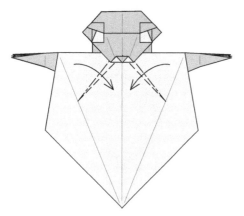

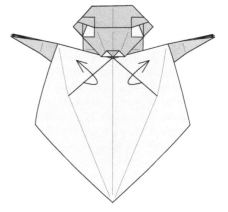

49. Form tiny pleats, allowing the top layer to become convex.

50. Pull around the top layer to the surface.

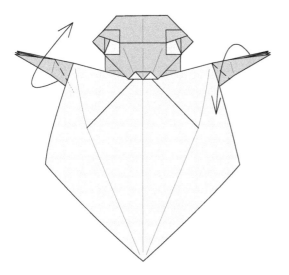

51. Valley fold the side flaps.

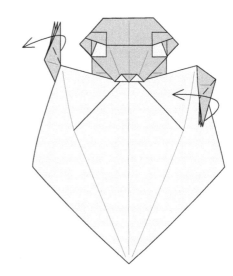

52. Valley fold the clusters of flaps over.

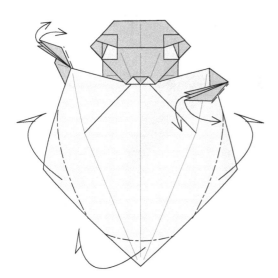

53. Spread apart the finger flaps. Shape the shell with mountain folds and round it out.

54. Completed *Dino Hatchling*.

Woolly Mammoth

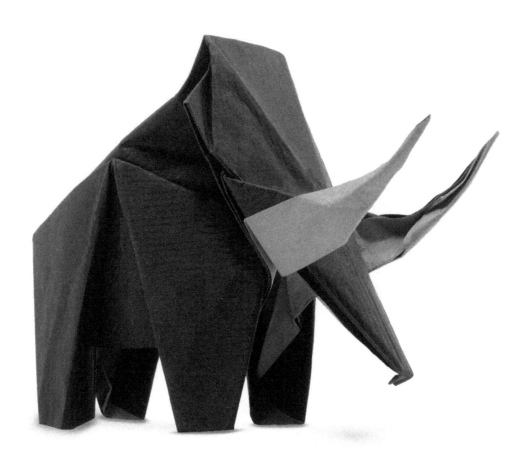

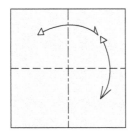

1. Precrease the sides in half with valley and mountain folds.

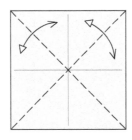

2. Precrease along the diagonals.

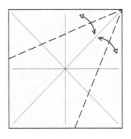

3. Precrease along the angle bisectors of one corner.

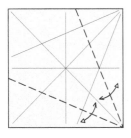

4. Precrease along the angle bisectors of an adjacent corner.

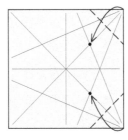

5. Valley fold the corners to the dotted intersections of creases.

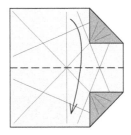

6. Valley fold in half.

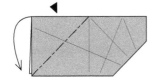

7. Reverse fold in half.

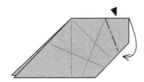

8. Reverse fold along the existing creases.

9. Swing over one flap.

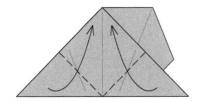

10. Valley fold the flaps to the top.

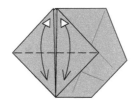

11. Precrease the flaps in half.

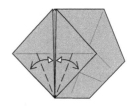

12. Precrease the flaps along the angle bisectors.

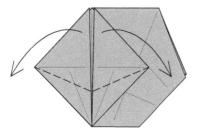

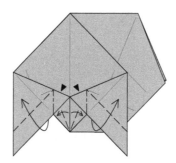

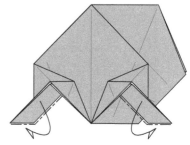

13. Valley fold the flaps outwards along the angle bisectors.

14. Valley fold the edges up, while swivel folding along the existing creases.

15. Wrap around a single layer at each side.

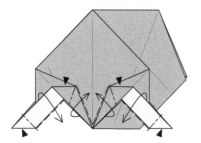

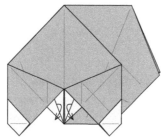

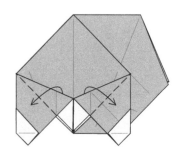

16. Open out the top layer at each side, lightly squash folding at the corners.

17. Pull out the trapped flap.

18. Swing the flaps down.

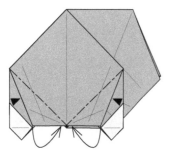

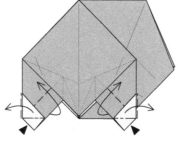

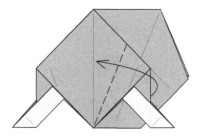

19. Reverse fold the flaps inside.

20. Valley fold the edges back up, squash folding the corners outwards. Allow hidden swivel folds to form.

21. Valley fold along the angle bisector.

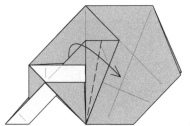

22. Valley fold outwards along the angle bisector.

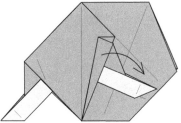

23. Unfold the pleat.

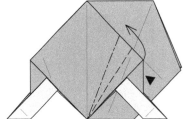

24. Reverse fold in and out along the existing creases.

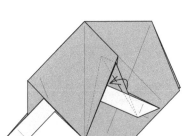

25. Valley fold the partial hidden edge as far as possible.

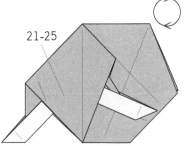

26. Repeat steps 21-25 in mirror image. Rotate the model slightly.

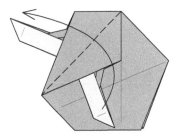

27. Swing the flap up.

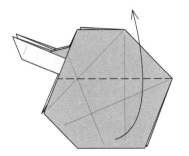

28. Valley fold the flap up.

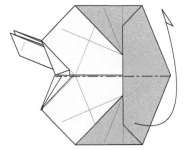

29. Mountain fold the lower section to match.

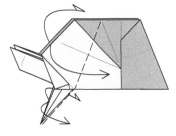

30. Valley fold the sides to the center, allowing an outside reverse fold to form.

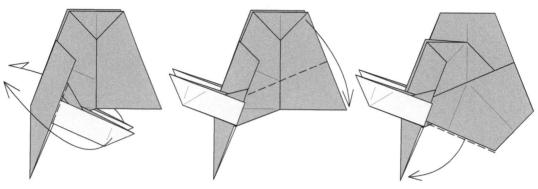

31. Valley fold the flaps over at each side.

32. Valley fold the top flap down so the corners meet.

33. Pull out a hidden layer, allowing the resulting edge to tuck into the flap at the left.

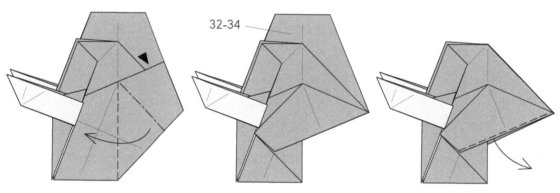

32-34

34. Squash fold the corner over.

35. Repeat steps 32-34 behind.

36. Pull out the middle hidden layer and flatten.

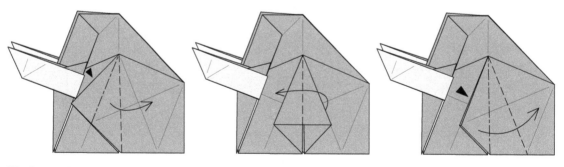

37. Squash fold the center flap.

38. Swing over one layer.

39. Squash fold the flap upwards.

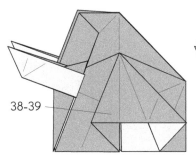

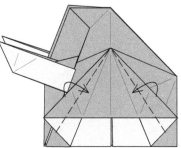

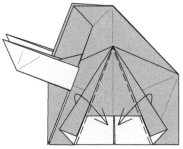

40. Repeat steps 38-39 in mirror image.

41. Valley fold along the angle bisectors.

42. Swing the flaps inwards.

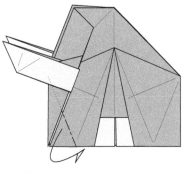

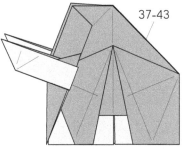

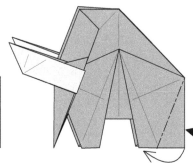

43. Mountain fold the trapped corner over.

44. Repeat steps 37-43 behind.

45. Reverse fold along the existing creases.

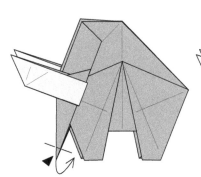

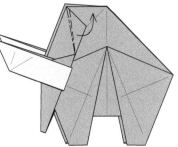

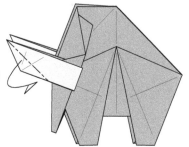

46. Reverse fold the tip of the flap.

47. Form a shallow pleat on the flap.

48. Mountain fold the corner.

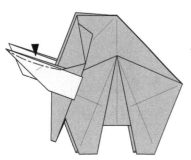

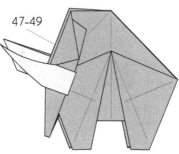

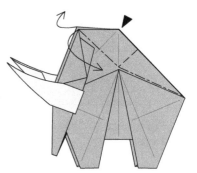

49. Round the top edge of the flap.

50. Repeat steps 47-49 behind.

51. Spread apart the sides of the head section while squash folding the model into a 3-D shape.

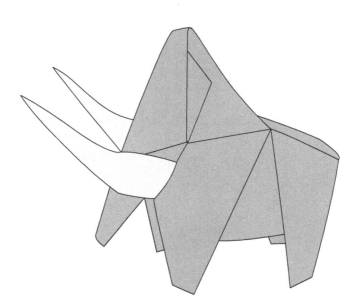

52. Completed *Woolly Mammoth*.

Dimetredon

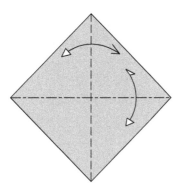

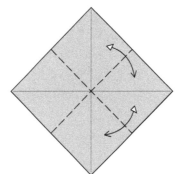

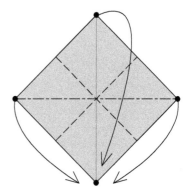

1. Precrease along the diagonals with a valley fold and a mountain fold.

2. Precrease the sides in half.

3. Bring the three corners to the bottom corner and collapse flat.

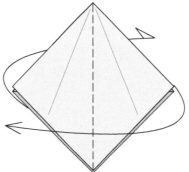

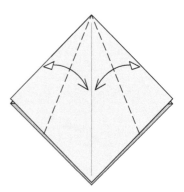

4. Valley fold the front and back flaps up.

5. Swing over a layer at each side.

6. Precrease the sides to the center.

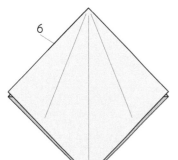

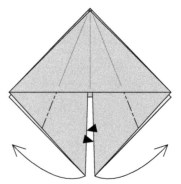

7. Repeat step 6 behind.

8. Swing over a layer at each side.

9. Reverse fold the flaps outwards.

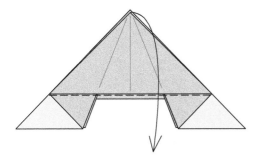

10. Swing down the top flap.

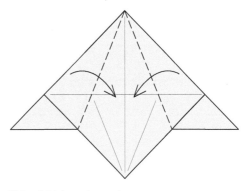

11. Valley fold the sides to the center.

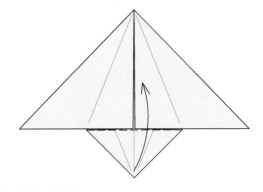

12. Valley fold the corner up.

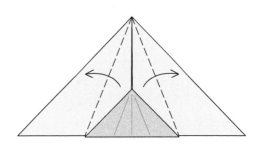

13. Swing the flaps back outwards.

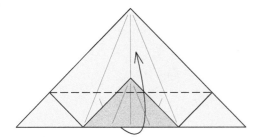

14. Valley fold the bottom edge up.

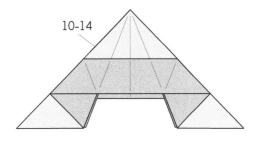

15. Repeat steps 10-14 behind.

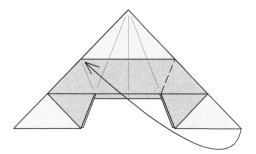

16. Valley fold the flap to align with the folded edge.

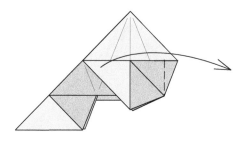

17. Valley fold the flap straight outwards.

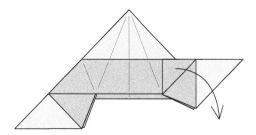

18. Unfold the pleat.

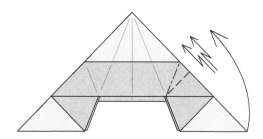

19. Crimp the flap along the existing creases.

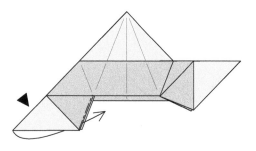

20. Undo the side reverse fold.

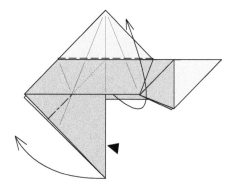

21. Open out along the middle while squash folding the bottom flap.

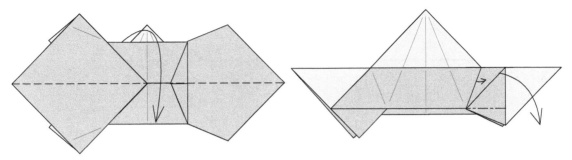

22. Swing the top section back down.

23 Slide the corner down, releasing the trapped paper.

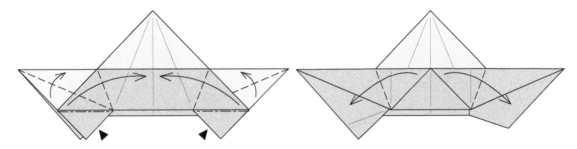

24. Squash fold the corners over.

25. Swing the flaps over.

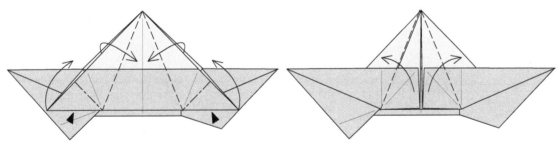

26. Valley fold the top layers to the center while squash folding the bottom flaps.

27. Swing the flaps outwards.

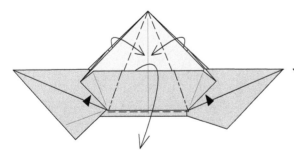

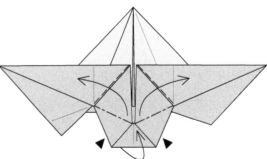

28. Pull the top single layer down while squash folding the sides to the center.

29. Squash fold the sides, bringing the top corners outwards.

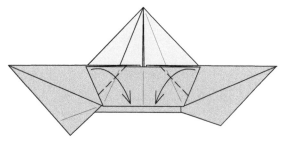

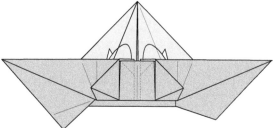

30. Valley fold the flaps down to the bottom edge.

31. Mountain fold the hidden corners to lock the layers together.

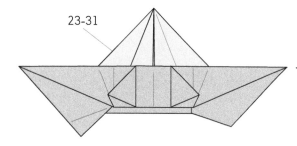

23-31

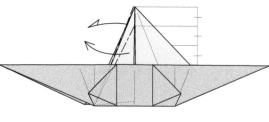

32. Repeat steps 23-31 behind.

33. Slide over a layer at each side, starting from the suggested 1/3rd division.

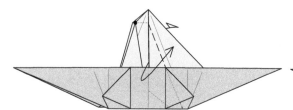

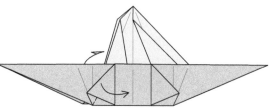

34. Reverse fold the outer layers, aligning with the suggested dotted intersection.

35. Undo the pleats at each side. Do *not* flatten the flaps.

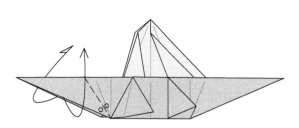

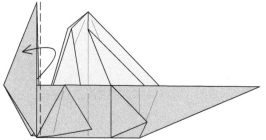

36. Outside reverse fold the flap along the indicated angle bisector.

37. Pull out a single layer and wrap it around.

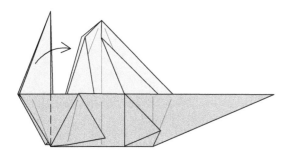

38. Valley fold the top layer over.

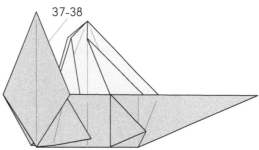

39. Repeat steps 37-38 behind.

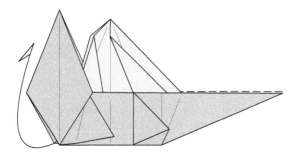

40. Spread apart the model along its center.

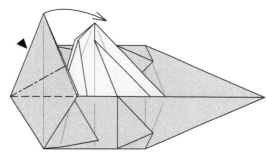

41. Squash fold the center flap.

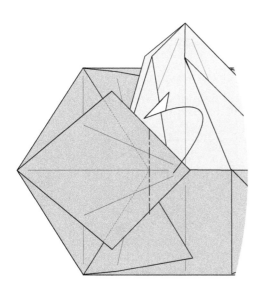

42. Mountain fold the corner to align with the hidden flaps below.

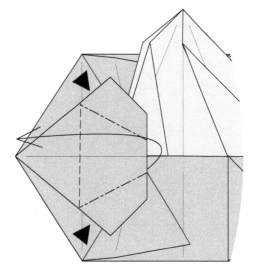

43. Valley fold the flap over while squash folding the sides.

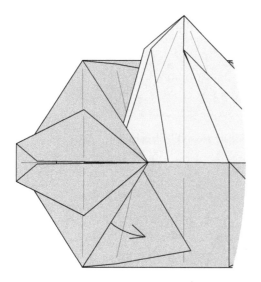

44. Pull out a single layer.

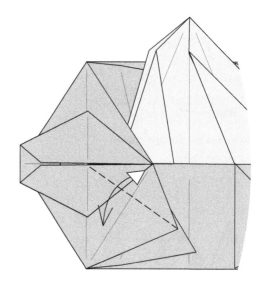

45. Lightly precrease the top layer.

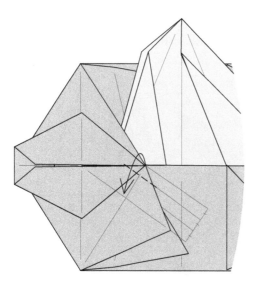

46. Valley fold the corner in along the indicated 1/3rd division.

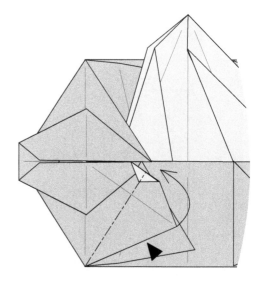

47. Reverse fold the side back inside.

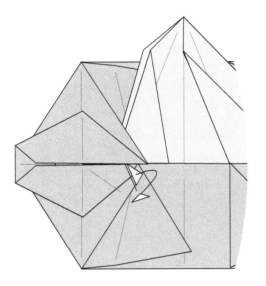

48. Mountain fold the corner.

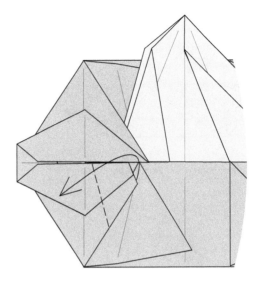

49. Valley fold the flap over so the side edges align.

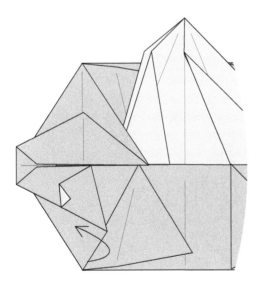

50. Tuck the corner under the flap.

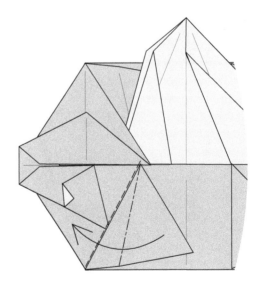

51. Reform the pleat on the top flap.

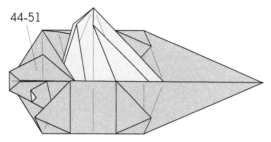

44-51

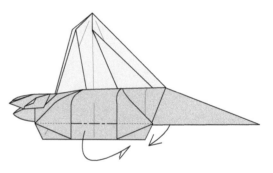

52. Repeat steps 44-51 on the top section.

53. Using soft folds, mountain fold the sides of the body down, crimping the hidden lower jaw down.

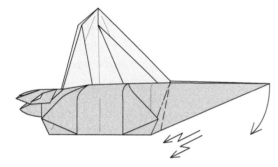

54. Crimp the tail flap down so its bottom edge lies straight.

55. Mountain fold the bottom edges inside.

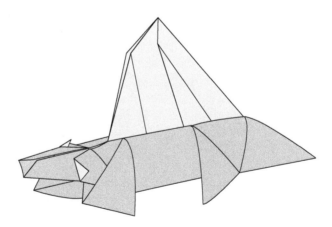

56. Completed *Dimetredon*.

Stegosaurus

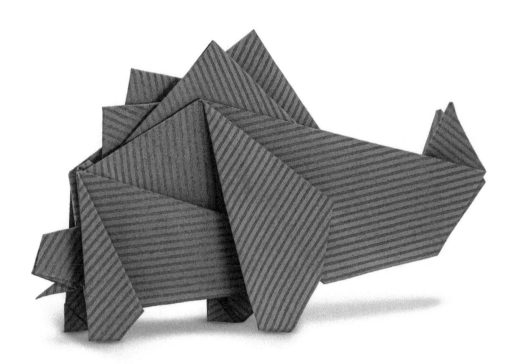

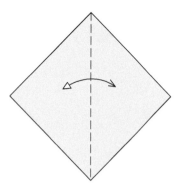

1. Precrease along the diagonal.

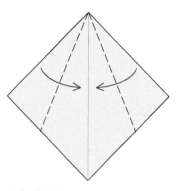

2. Valley fold the sides to the center.

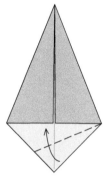

3. Valley fold the bottom edge up.

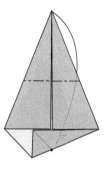

4. Mountain fold towards the dotted point.

5. Unfold at the bottom.

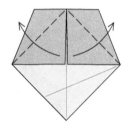

6. Valley fold the corners outwards.

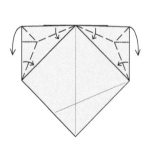

7. Rabbit ear the corners down.

8. Swing the flap up from behind.

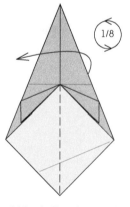

9. Valley fold in half and rotate the model.

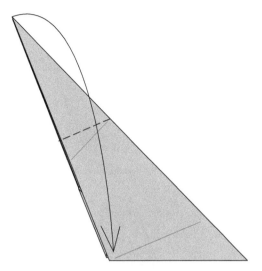

10. Valley fold down.

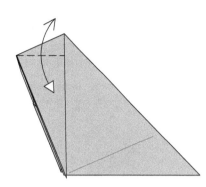

11. Precrease.

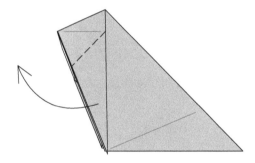

12. Valley fold up towards the crease.

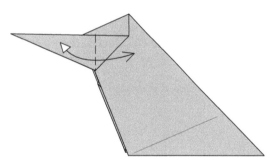

13. Precrease again.

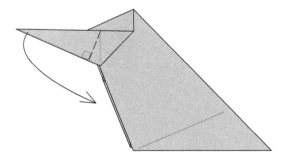

14. Valley fold over, starting from the last crease.

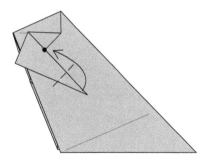

15. Valley fold the corner to the dotted intersection.

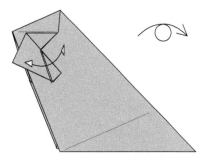

16. Precrease along the folded edge and turn over.

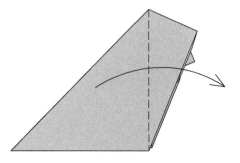

17. Valley fold over.

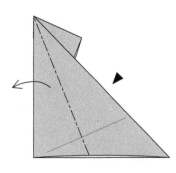

18. Spread squash the flap down.

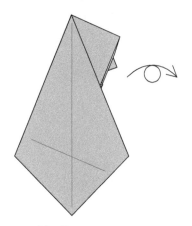

19. Turn over.

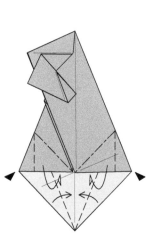

20. Reverse fold the sides.

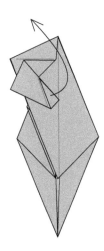

21. Open out the pleats.

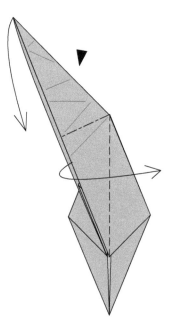

22. Spread apart the layers evenly and squash the flap down.

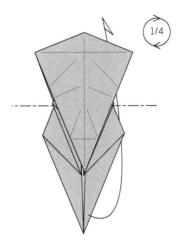

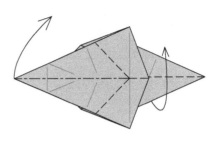

23. Mountain fold the flaps behind at the narrowest point. Rotate the model.

24. Valley fold in half while reverse folding along the exiting creases.

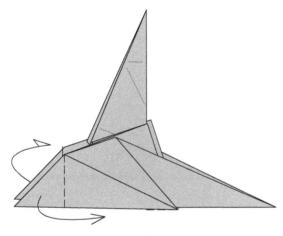

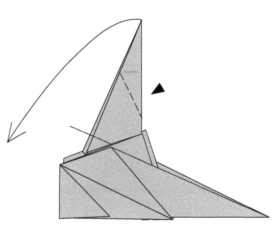

25. Valley fold the two front flaps.

26. Reverse fold in and out along the existing creases.

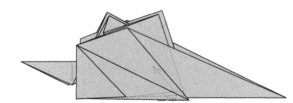

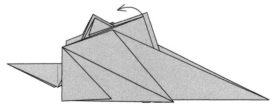

27. Valley fold a small bit of the hidden edge up - this will help with the next step.

28. Slide the top flap towards the left.

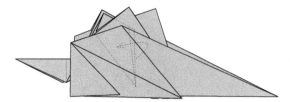

29. Valley fold a small bit of the hidden edge up - this will help with the next step.

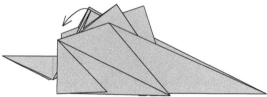

30. Slide the top flap towards the left.

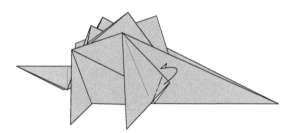

31. Valley fold the flaps down.

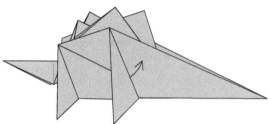

32. Pull out a single layer.

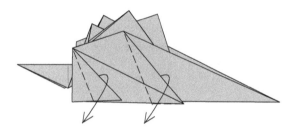

33. Mountain fold.

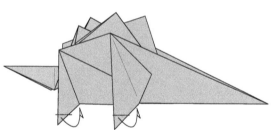

34. Mountain fold the corners behind.

31-34

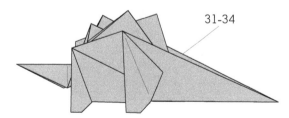

35. Repeat steps 31-34 behind.

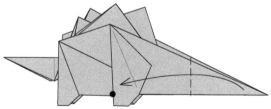

36. Valley fold towards the dotted point.

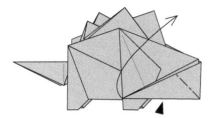

37. Spread squash the flap up.

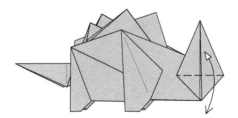

38. Precrease the flap.

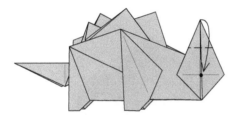

39. Valley fold towards the crease.

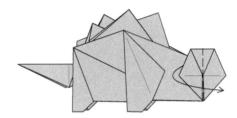

40. Valley fold the flap in half.

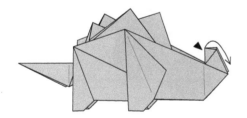

41. Reverse fold.

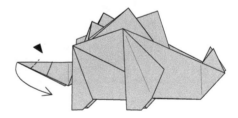

42. Reverse fold in and then out.

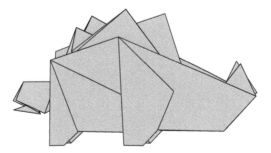

43. Completed *Stegosaurus*.

Triceratops

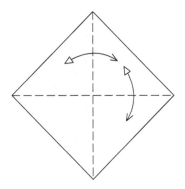

1. Precrease along the diagonals.

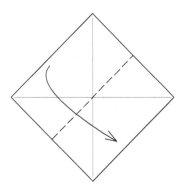

2. Valley fold in half.

3. Valley fold the corner over to hit the edge.

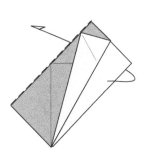

4. Open out the back layer.

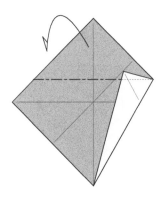

5. Mountain fold the top corner behind.

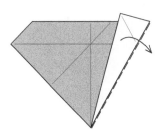

6. Open out the side.

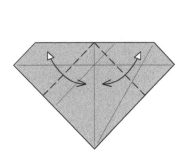

7. Precrease to the center.

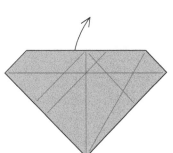

8. Open out completely.

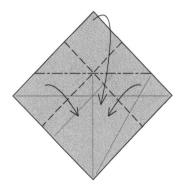

9. Collapse down using the existing creases.

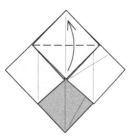

10. Valley fold up.

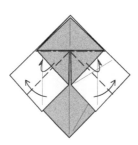

11. Valley fold the sides outwards, while reverse folding the triangular sections under.

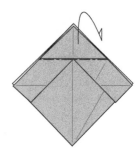

12. Mountain fold the top section.

13. Turn over.

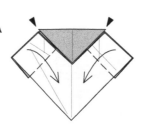

14. Valley fold the sides inwards, reverse folding at the corners.

15. Swing one flap over.

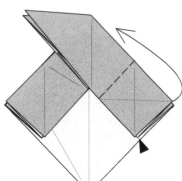

16. Fold over the top layer, allowing a squash fold to form.

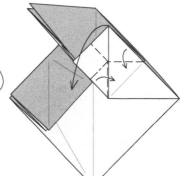

17. Rabbit ear the top flap.

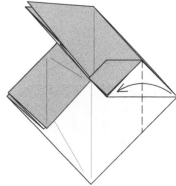

18. Valley fold the corner inwards.

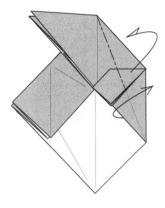

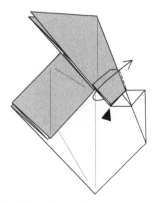

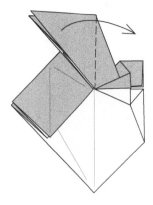

19. Mountain fold the edge behind, allowing the bottom flap to flip outwards.

20. Swing the top flap outwards, squashing the corner flap to allow it to flatten.

21. Swing the top flap back over.

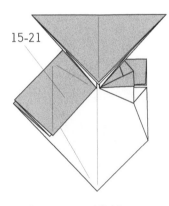

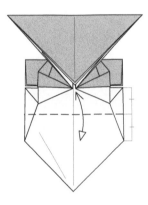

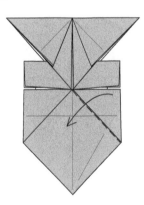

22. Repeat steps 15-21 in mirror image.

23. Precrease in half and then turn over.

24. Open out the top flap.

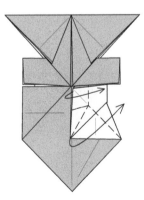

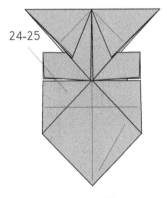

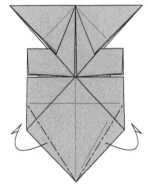

25. Swing the top flap back over while folding the top single layer towards the side edge.

26. Repeat steps 24-25 in mirror image.

27. Mountain fold the edges behind.

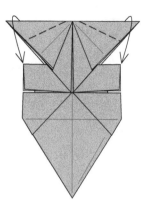

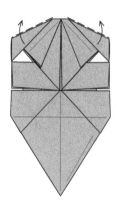

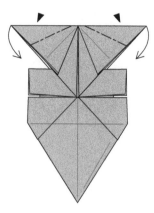

28. Valley fold towards the corners of the flaps.

29. Unfold.

30. Reverse fold down, distributing the layers with one at the top and two at the bottom.

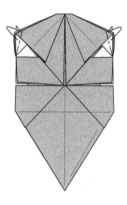

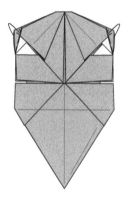

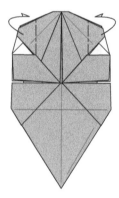

31. Mountain fold the top layers in along the angle trisectors.

32. Valley fold the remaining edges in to match.

33. Mountain fold the sides behind..

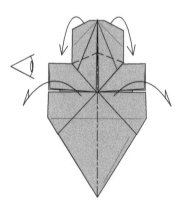

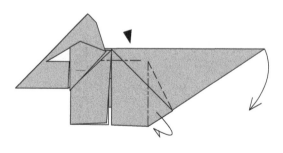

34. Lightly mountain fold in half while outside reverse folding the front.

35. Crimp the flap down while rounding out the top edge.

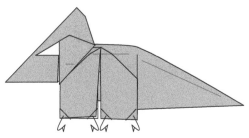

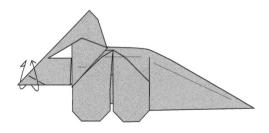

36. Mountain fold the corners in and repeat behind.

37. Outside reverse fold the tip.

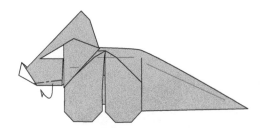

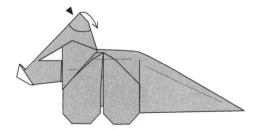

38. Mountain fold a small amount of the lower edges inside.

39. Push in the top edge and round out the head.

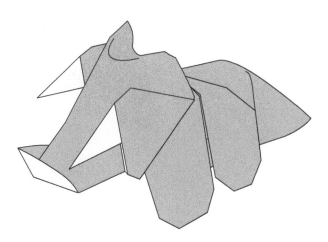

40. Completed *Triceratops*.

Ankylosaurus

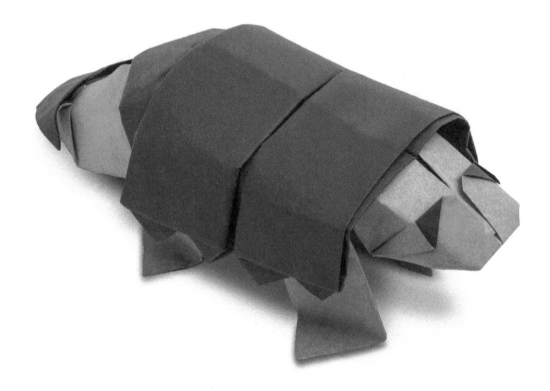

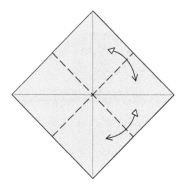

1. Precrease along the diagonals using valley folds and mountain folds.

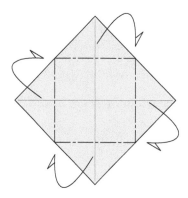

2. Precrease the sides in half.

3. Mountain fold the four corners to the center.

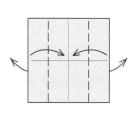

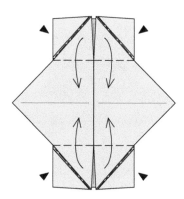

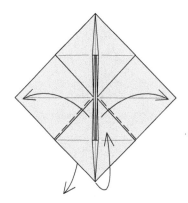

4. Valley fold the sides inwards, allowing the flaps from behind to swing forward.

5. Squash fold the four corners inwards.

6. Stretch the flaps towards the outer corners, allowing the flap from behind to come to the front.

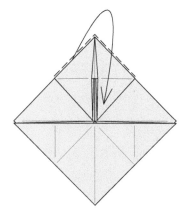

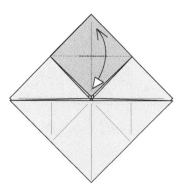

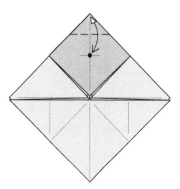

7. Wrap around a single layer from behind.

8. Pinch the top layer in half.

9. Precrease towards the dotted intersection.

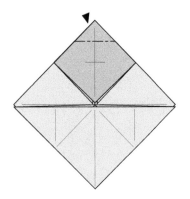

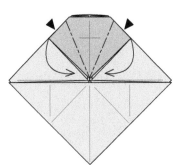

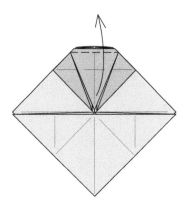

10. Sink the top corner.

11. Reverse fold the sides along the angle bisectors.

12. Swing the top flap up.

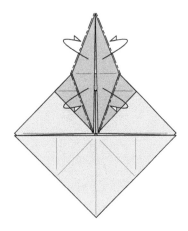

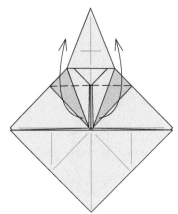

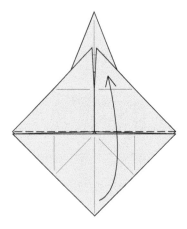

13. Wrap around a single layer at each side.

14. Swing the flaps up.

15. Swing the top layer up.

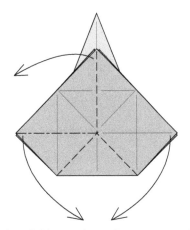

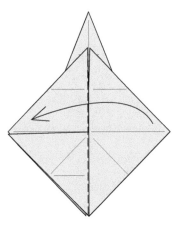

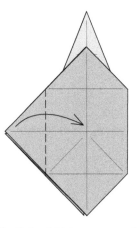

16. Rabbit ear the top layer.

17. Swing over a single layer.

18. Valley fold the corner to the center.

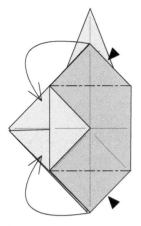

19. Reverse fold the corners.

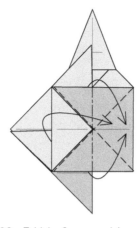

20. Fold the flap over while reverse folding the sides.

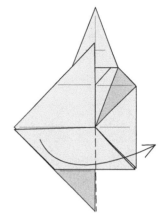

21. Swing over the center flap.

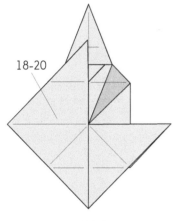

22. Repeat steps 18-20 in mirror image.

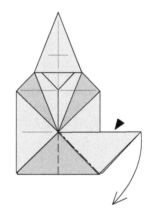

23. Squash fold the center flap down.

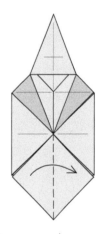

24. Swing over one layer.

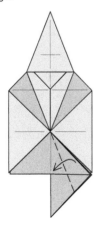

25. Valley fold along the angle bisector.

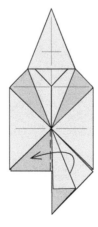

26. Swing the flap back over.

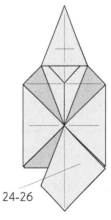

27. Repeat steps 24-26 in mirror image.

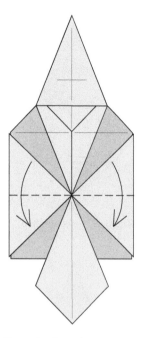

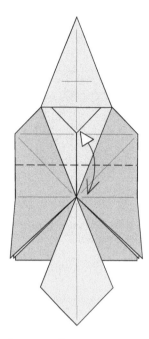

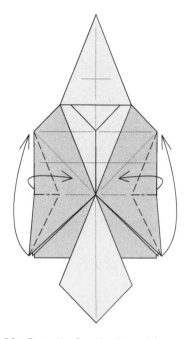

28. Swing the flaps down.

29. Precrease the top section in half through all layers.

30. Swing the flaps back up while incorporating reverse folds.

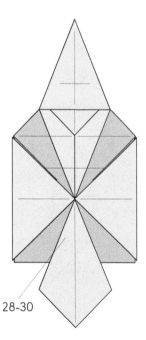

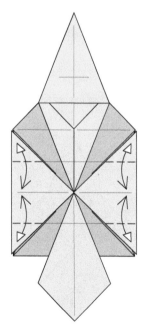

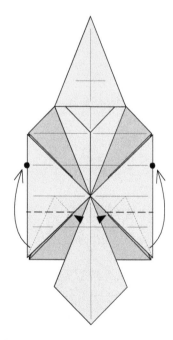

28-30

31. Repeat steps 28-30 on the bottom.

32. Precrease the top flap in half.

33. Valley fold the corners to the dotted intersections, allowing tiny squash folds to form.

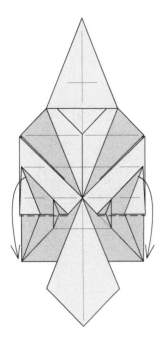

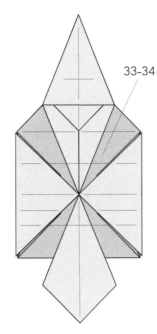

33-34

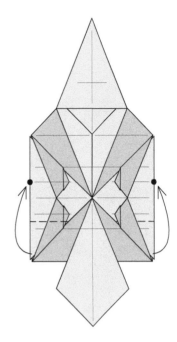

34. Swing the flaps down.

35. Repeat steps 33-34 at the top.

36. Valley fold the corners to the dotted intersections.

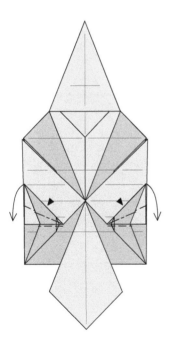

36-37

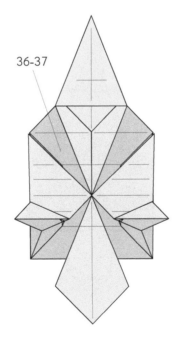

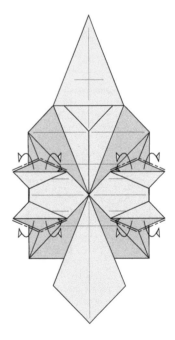

37. Squash fold the flaps over.

38. Repeat steps 36-37 at the top.

39. Wrap around all of the layers on each flap.

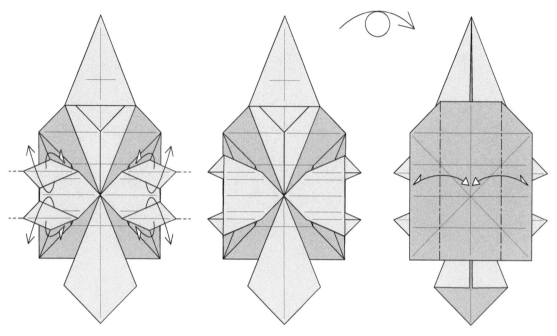

40. Flip the four flaps behind.

41. Turn over.

42. Precrease the sides with mountain folds through all of the layers.

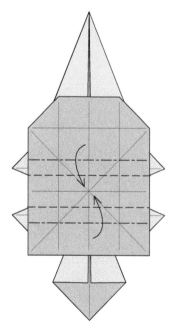

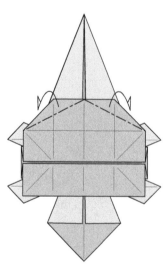

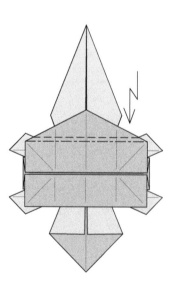

43. Pleat the top sections towards the center.

44. Mountain fold the corners inside.

45. Form a shallow pleat.

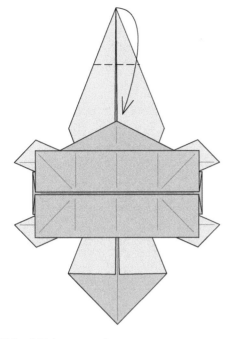

46. Valley fold the corner down.

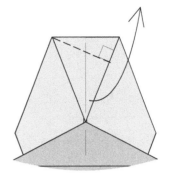

47. Valley fold the flap up so the side edges align.

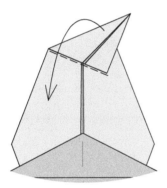

48. Swing the flap down.

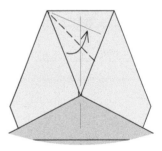

49. Valley fold towards the crease.

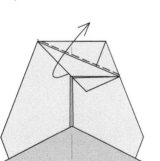

50. Pull around a single layer and flatten.

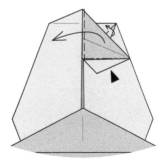

51. Squash fold the center flap.

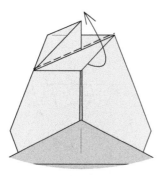

52. Pull around a single layer and flatten.

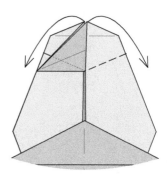

53. Spread open the top flaps and flatten.

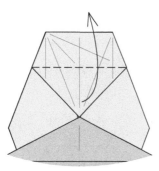

54. Valley fold the corner up.

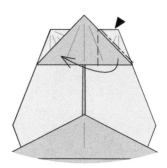

55. Valley fold the flap over, allowing a spread squash to form.

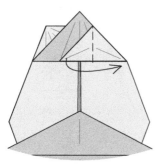

56. Valley fold the flap back over.

55-56

57. Repeat steps 55-56 in mirror image.

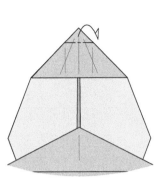

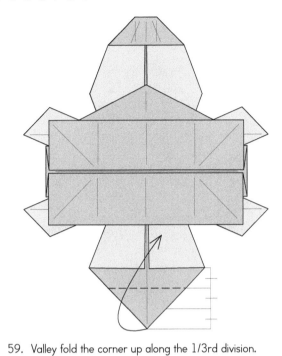

58. Mountain fold the corner around the hidden edge.

59. Valley fold the corner up along the 1/3rd division.

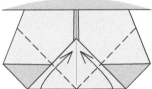

60. Valley fold the sides to the center.

61. Valley fold the corners down at a slight taper.

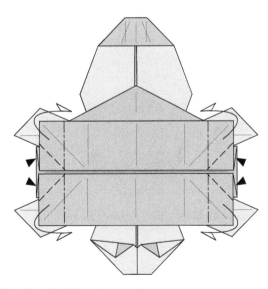

62. Mountain fold a little bit of the corner.

63. Swivel fold the edges inside.

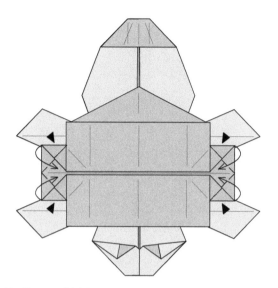

64. Reverse fold the corners at each side.

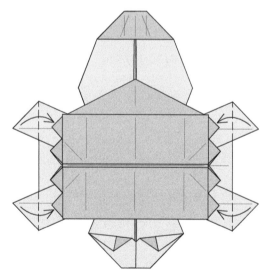

65. Mountain fold the corners inside.

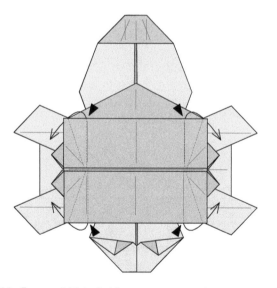

66. Reverse fold the hidden corners outwards.

67. Valley fold the flaps inwards.

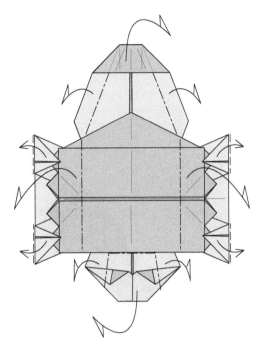

68. Fold down the sides of the body, tail, and head.
    Open out the feet.

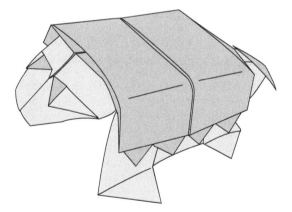

69. Completed *Ankylosaurus*.

T-rex Skeleton

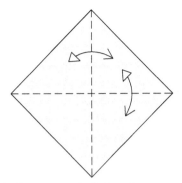

1. Precrease in half along the diagonals.

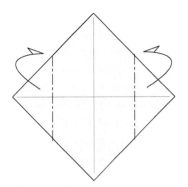

2. Mountain fold the sides behind.

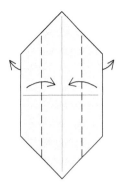

3. Valley fold the sides to the center, allowing the back flaps to flip forward.

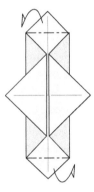

4. Mountain fold the corners behind.

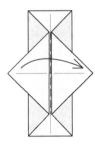

5. Swing a flap over.

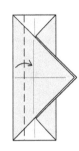

6. Valley fold to the center.

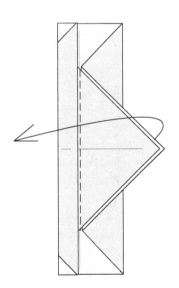

7. Swing both flaps over.

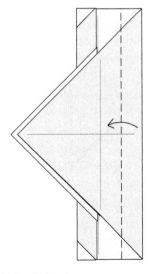

8. Valley fold to the center.

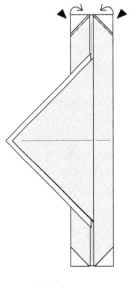

9. Reverse fold the corners.

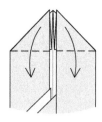

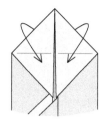

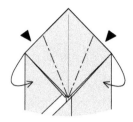

10.   Swing down the flaps.

11.   Wrap around a single layer from behind.

12.   Reverse fold the sides.

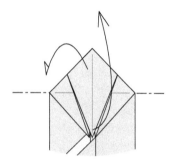

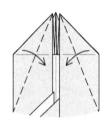

9-14

13.   Flip the cluster of flaps up, and the top point down.

14.   Valley fold the sides to the center.

15.   Repeat steps 9-14 at the bottom.

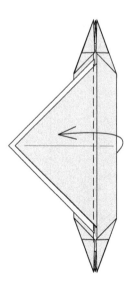

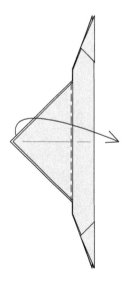

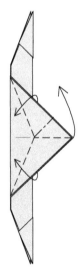

16.   Valley fold.

17.   Valley fold both layers over.

18.   Rabbit ear, treating both layers as one.

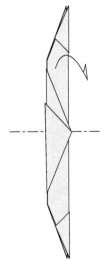

19. Mountain fold along the center.

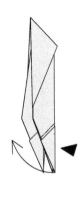

20. Reverse fold through.

21. Reverse fold the hidden flap down.

22. Precrease.

23. Pinch the flaps in half and spread them apart.

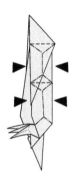

24. Pinch the two sections in half.

25. Repeat steps 20-24 on the other side.

20-24

26. Completed leg section.

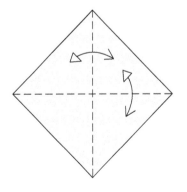

27. Begin with another square. Precrease in half.

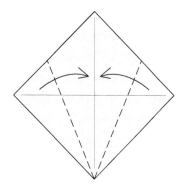

28. Valley fold to the center.

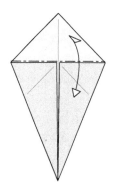

29. Precrease with a mountain fold.

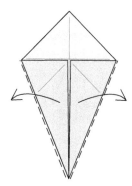

30. Unfold.

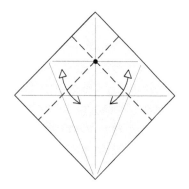

31. Precrease through the indicated intersection.

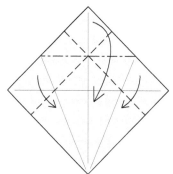

32. Collapse down along the existing creases.

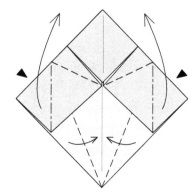

33. Squash fold the side flaps upwards.

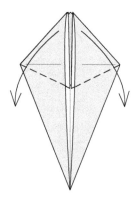

34. Swing the flaps down.

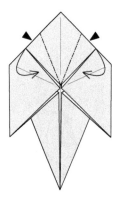

35. Reverse fold the sides.

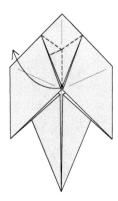

36. Rabbit ear the top flap.

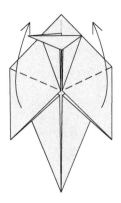

37. Swing the flaps back up.

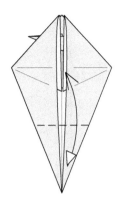

38. Precrease the bottom.

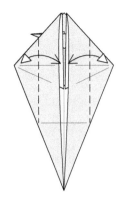

39. Precrease the sides.

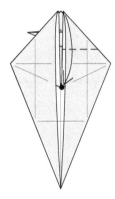

40. Valley fold towards the indicated crease.

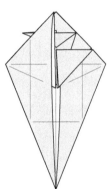

41. Turn over.

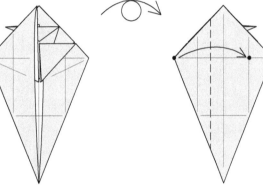

42. Valley fold to the indicated crease.

Small Flap

43. Tuck the indicated small flap underneath the top layer.

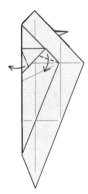

44. Swivel fold over as far as possible.

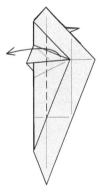

45. Valley fold along the center.

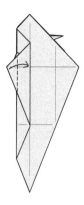

46. Valley fold to the center.

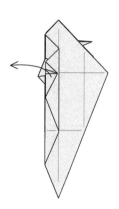

47. Unfold the pleat.

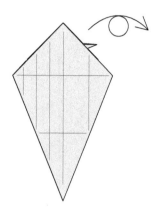

48. Turn over.

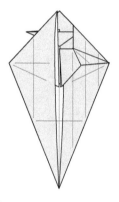

49. Repeat steps 40-48 in mirror image.

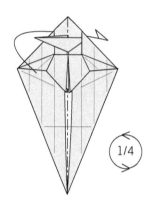

50. Mountain fold in half and rotate.

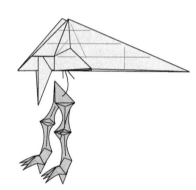

51. Tuck the leg section into the uppermost pocket.

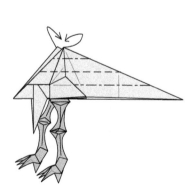

52. Replace the pleats to lock the two sections together.

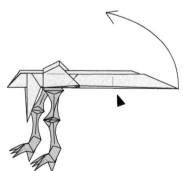

53. Reverse fold the flap up.

54. Reverse fold down.

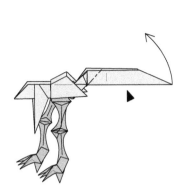

55. Reverse fold up.

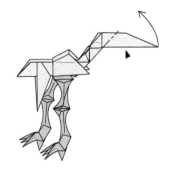

56. Reverse fold down.

57. Reverse fold up.

58. Reverse fold down.

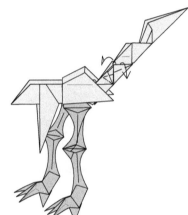

59. Valley fold the sides down, swivel folding the small corners over.

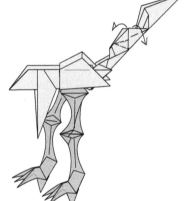

60. Swivel fold the sides again.

61. Swivel fold again.

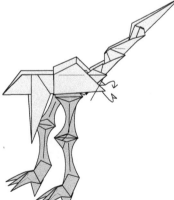

62. Mountain fold the corners.

63. Reverse fold.

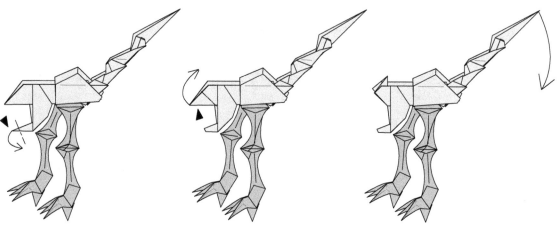

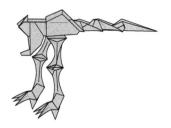

64. Reverse fold the tip.

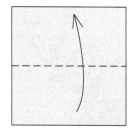

65. Reverse fold.

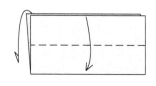

66. Pull the tail section down.

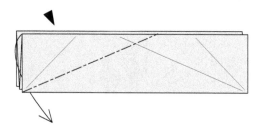

67. Completed rear section.

68. Begin with another square. Valley fold up.

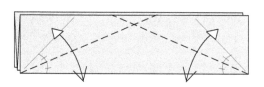

69. Valley fold the sides down.

70. Precrease the corners.

71. Bring the creases to the bottom edge to precrease.

72. Reverse fold.

73. Closed reverse fold (symmetry of the inner layers is not critical).

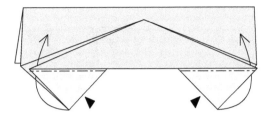

74. Reverse fold the corners up.

75. Reverse fold the corners down.

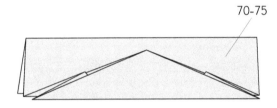

70-75

76. Repeat steps 70-75 behind.

77. Open out along the center.

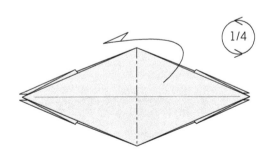

1/4

78. Mountain fold. Rotate the model.

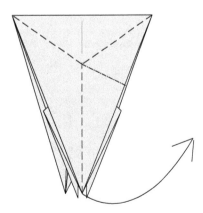

79. Rabbit ear the top section.

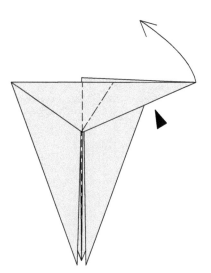

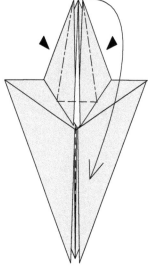

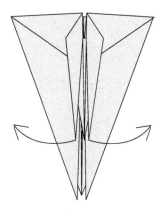

80. Squash fold the cluster of flaps up.

81. Petal fold the cluster of flaps down.

82. Pull the side flaps outwards slightly.

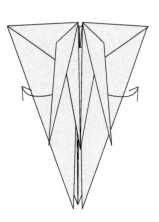

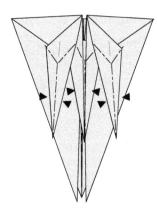

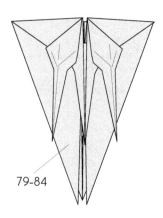

83. Slide out two layers from each side.

84. Pinch the flaps in half.

85. Repeat steps 79-84 behind.

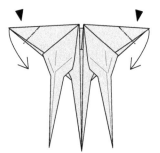

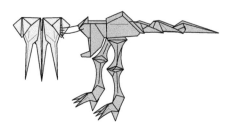

86. Squash fold the corners down.

87. Tuck the flaps from the rear section into the pockets.

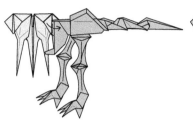

88.   Swing over the flap.

89.   Completed body section.

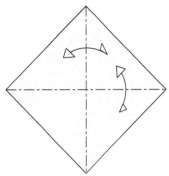

90.   Begin with another square. Precrease with mountain folds.

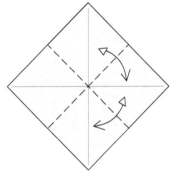

91.   Precrease with valley folds.

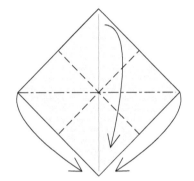

92.   Collapse down.

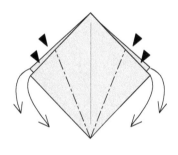

93.   Reverse fold the sides.

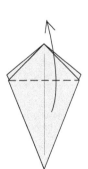

94.   Swing the top flap up.

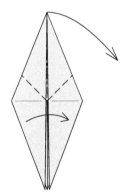

95.   Swing one flap over while incorporating a reverse fold.

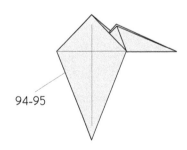

94-95

96.   Repeat steps 94-95 behind.

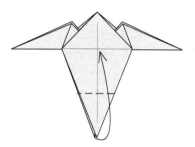

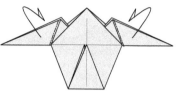

97. Valley fold the flaps up to the crease.

98. Mountain fold the sides behind.

99. Valley fold, allowing the flaps from behind to swing forward.

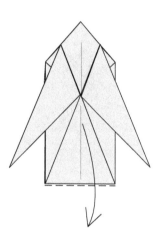

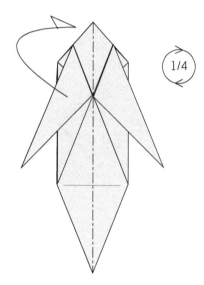

1/4

100. Swing down the two flaps.

101. Mountain fold in half and rotate.

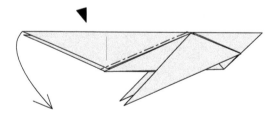

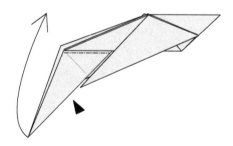

102. Reverse fold down.

103. Reverse fold up.

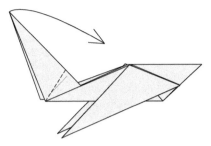

104.   Valley fold to the bottom edge.

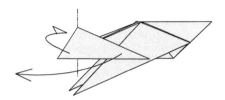

105.   Mountain fold along the indicated axis.

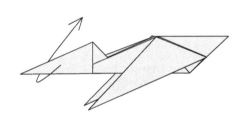

106.   Unfold the pleat.

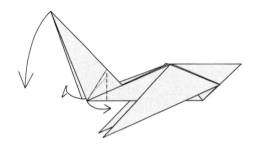

107.   Crimp down along the existing creases.

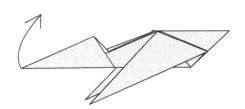

108.   Unfold the crimp.

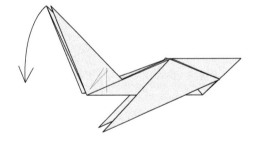

109.   Pull the center flap through.

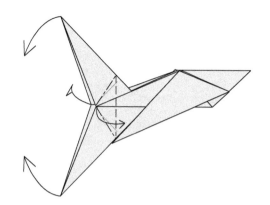

110.   Crimp both flaps simultaneously.

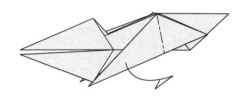

111.   Mountain fold.

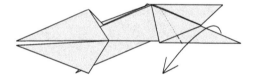

112.   Valley fold.

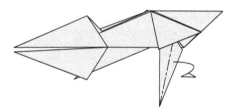

113.   Mountain fold.

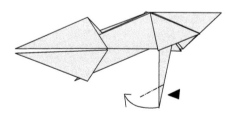

114.   Reverse fold.

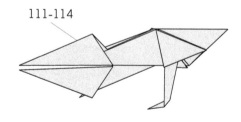

111-114

115.   Repeat steps 111-114 behind.

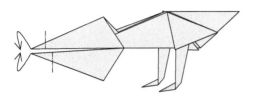

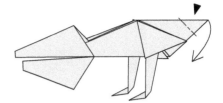

116. Reverse fold the tips.

117. Reverse fold.

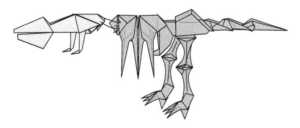

118. Lock the two sections together.
Open out the head. You can form
a stand by bending thin wire.

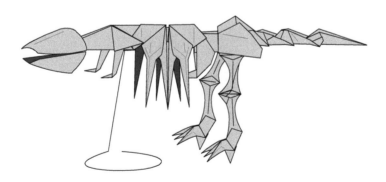

119. Completed *T-rex Skeleton*.

CPSIA information can be obtained
at www.ICGtesting.com
Printed in the USA
BVHW051647080222
628393BV00002B/17